Adults ICT Skills

 TH

# Teaching Adults ICT Skills

**Dr Alan Clarke**

Learning Matters

First published in 2006 by Learning Matters Ltd

*British Library Cataloguing in Publication Data*
A CIP record for this book is available from the British Library.

ISBN-13: 978 1 84445 040 4
ISBN-10: 1 84445 040 6

Cover design by Topics – The Creative Partnership
Project management by Deer Park Productions
Typeset by PDQ Typesetting Ltd
Printed and bound in Great Britain by Bell & Bain Ltd, Glasgow

Learning Matters Ltd
33 Southernhay East
Exeter EXI INX
Tel: 01392 215560
Email: info@learningmatters.co.uk
*www.learningmatters.co.uk*

# CONTENTS

Dr Alan Clarke is Associate Director for ICT and Learning at the National Institute of Adult Continuing Education (NIACE) and is also an Open University teacher. Before moving to the NIACE, he worked for the National Council for Educational Technology (now BECTA) and the UK government's Department for Education and Skills in the Learning Technology Unit. Alan has been involved with ICT and computer-based learning for over 20 years and has undertaken a wide range of investigations, research studies and evaluations. His doctorate was on the design of computer-based learning materials. He is currently a member of the DfES Standards Unit expert group on ICT and the DfES ICT Skill for Life partners group.

# ACKNOWLEDGEMENTS

To my wife for her help and support during the writing of the book.

The author and publisher wish to acknowledge the following for use of on-screen images: CorelDRAW, e-Skills UK, NIACE, bksb (West Nottinghamshire College) and the Microsoft Corporation.

Screen shots reprinted with permission of Microsoft Corporation.

Screen shots are copyright Corel Corporation and Corel Corporation Limited, reprinted by permission.

Microsoft and Corel trademarks are acknowledged.

The author and publisher wish to acknowledge Hodder Education for their agreement to reproduce an exercise from their Level I New Clait 2006 book.

This book is aimed at teachers, tutors and trainers of ICT user skills working in colleges, workplaces and the community. A large proportion of these are part-time. Many have more than one education or training employer while others are working within Information Technology in various roles such as technician, software engineer and web designer. The background of teachers, trainers and tutors of ICT varies widely, with many transferring from other disciplines.

Learners anticipate that their ICT courses will be practical and the vast majority of programmes take place in some type of workshop environment with learners working on personal computers. In some cases, learners are attending learning or drop-in centres where they can work on their own with some tutorial support while others choose to attend more formal provision. In all settings there are some unique features that make ICT teaching and training different from other subjects, the principal one being the use of a computer. In addition the nature of ICT requires an individual to acquire certain personal skills. These factors tend to encourage courses to focus on the individual and this often results in group or whole class learning methods being neglected. This seriously limits methods that many learners find beneficial and forces too narrow a range to be employed.

*Teaching Adults ICT Skills* offers advice on a wide range of methods and demonstrates how to employ approaches that are now widely accepted as good practice.

## Introduction

The growth in the use of information and communication technology (ICT) has been rapid. Many hundreds of thousands of people take part in ICT courses each year, reflecting the impact that technology has had on people's employment and lives. The government (2003) has acknowledged the importance of ICT by making it a Skill for Life alongside literacy, numeracy and language; that is, a fundamental skill. The majority of both existing and new jobs require ICT skills and knowledge. In addition, technology is having an increasing influence on education, government and community. E-learning is developing quickly, with many opportunities to learn now available through the use of technology. These are only available to learners who are competent and confident users of ICT. Without these skills, they are effectively excluded from such opportunities. Government has set significant targets to provide services and information online, demonstrating again that ICT is fundamental to participating in society. In everyday activities people have discovered the benefits of online shopping, digital cameras, planning journeys, helping their children with homework and numerous other advantages of being computer literate.

These changes are continuing and accelerating (Clarke and Englebright, 2003). The need for higher levels of ICT skills is already apparent amongst many employers, and the trend is for more advanced skills (Gartner, 2004) to be required. All employees are going to need to upgrade their ICT skills and to accept that skills which were the preserve of the ICT professional are now needed by all users. This trend, combined with the need to cope with an ever-changing range of ICT applications and systems, means that users will need to be able to adapt to new situations. For new users – and there is a considerable proportion of the population with no or very limited skills – then the initial step is quite high. A Department for Education and Skills survey reported that 53% of adults had very limited ICT practical skills (DfES, 2003).

Many organisations have made substantial investments in ICT in order to improve their efficiency and effectiveness. They have identified that access to and use of information is a key part of their operation. The skills, attitudes and knowledge of the staff employing the technology are vital to the realisation of the benefits ICT can bring to an organisation. Initial and continuing training of staff is therefore a critical priority.

The background to providing ICT skills and knowledge is characterised by:

- continuous change linked to the need to update skills and knowledge;
- the need to be able to transfer skills to new situations;

- using ICT in a range of contexts (e.g. work, leisure, community, society and learning);
- initial experience to provide a sound foundation for future learning;
- the desire to realise the value of major investments in ICT by organisations.

# Motivation

There have been several surveys and other investigations into the reasons why people want to learn to use ICT. Some of the main reasons are (Prime Minister's Strategy Unit, 2005):

- employment (e.g. financial records);
- supporting learners' learning;
- supporting the education of learners' children;
- accessing government online services (e.g. Inland Revenue Self Assessment);
- shopping online;
- communication with family and friends;
- hobbies and interests (e.g. digital photography);
- finding information.

Learners will have their own mixture of needs and desires which will include some of these reasons. It is clearly vital that these are assessed so that the learning programme can be successfully targeted. The ICT Skill for Life standard places an emphasis on learning in a purposeful way, that is, the ICT programme should be focused on the learners' needs and interests.

As well as understanding what are the main reasons that learners have for undertaking ICT courses, it is also useful to understand the factors that discourage people from taking part. Even learners who enrol on a course may well share some of these misgivings. Some of the negatives factors are that they:

- cannot see the relevance of technology to themselves;
- cannot identify the benefits of technology to themselves;
- lack confidence in their ability to learn about technology;
- have concerns about security of technology;
- have concerns about unsuitable content on the Internet.

Lack of relevance and a lack of confidence are major concerns of many non-ICT users and so it is useful to address them during learning programmes. Activities need to meet learners' needs so they can readily see that they are learning skills that will help them. Gaining confidence is often associated with success so learners need to be assisted to succeed and have their success acknowledged.

# Ongoing ICT education and training

The dynamic nature of ICT, combined with employers' demands for staff with more advanced computer skills, leads to the need for users to continually develop their skills and understanding. Even users who are largely motivated by personal reasons to learn to use ICT will often identify new areas that they want to exploit. Many users will therefore return for more advanced education and training, and everyone will need to be able to cope with some degree of change. Being able to undertake self development and to transfer skills to new situations are vital parts of ICT learning.

Many organisations have invested in e-learning and other forms of self development which are available to employees and learners in learning centres. These can take a variety of forms including online centres accessed over Intranets or through virtual learning environments to large physical centres where people can drop in to study. In all cases, the critical issue is the rate of successful completion of the learning pro-grammes. It is often very low with many people motivated to begin with but quickly dropping out. Learners who are able to succeed in these types of environments are often characterised by being (Simpson, 2000; Clarke, 2002; Learning and Skills Development Agency, 2001):

- highly motivated;
- confident;
- successful learners (i.e. with well-developed learning skills).

The success of learning centres or other self-study approaches is often dependent on learners being provided with:

- assistance with developing learning skills;
- appropriate support (e.g. technical, mentoring, coaching and tutoring);
- an environment that encourages peer support.

It is clear that even students with basic ICT skills who are seeking to enhance them may well find self-study a challenge unless adequate support is provided. Learning centres can be a very successful approach providing they are structured to support the learner and that the study materials are of high quality.

# User profiles

It is clear that users' needs for ICT skills and knowledge vary depending on the type of technology and its application. The needs of teachers seeking to use ICT to support their teaching may well demand very sophisticated skills in searching the World Wide Web or with using presentation applications, while requiring only basic skills in using databases. Researchers may well need to be able to construct databases to enable them to analyse research data. A secretary will need advanced word-proces-sing, spreadsheet and communication skills but may never need to use a presentation application. The users' needs and role will determine the level of skills and understanding they require.

ICT programmes are often designed with the assumption that the users all need the same level of expertise. There may be some choice in a modular course but often little in terms of level. Tutors will be aware that learners attending intermediary or advanced level courses will often have very advanced skills in particular areas due to their work or interests, while having relatively underdeveloped skills in other areas. This is sometimes called a spiky profile and is probably the norm for many users. Figure I shows an example of a spiky profile in terms of the different levels. Figure 2 shows the profile of a group of new computer users in terms of their initial input skills (e.g. mouse and keyboard). Even new users' skills often vary.

It is sometimes argued that new ICT users will need to have a basic introduction to everything so that they have a good foundation for later development and this has a certain truth. However, even beginners will have different needs and aspirations. The key is to be aware of the learners' needs and current skills.

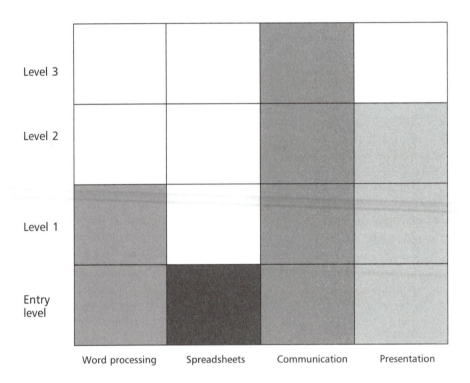

Fig. I Example outline profile

| Learners | Point and click devices (e.g. mouse) | | | Keyboard | | | |
|---|---|---|---|---|---|---|---|
| | Pointer position | Clicking left and right buttons | Drag and drop | Enter letters and numbers | Delete and backspace | Special keys (e.g. PrtSc) | Short cuts |
| Carol | 2 | 2 | 1 | 2 | 2 | 1 | 1 |
| Janet | 3 | 2 | 2 | 3 | 3 | 1 | 1 |
| Laura | 4 | 3 | 3 | 3 | 3 | 2 | 2 |
| George | 2 | 1 | 1 | 2 | 1 | 1 | 1 |
| Sabal | 5 | 4 | 4 | 4 | 3 | 3 | 2 |
| Linda | 2 | 3 | 2 | 2 | 2 | 2 | 1 |
| John | 2 | 2 | 2 | 2 | 1 | 1 | 1 |
| William | 3 | 3 | 3 | 3 | 2 | 2 | 1 |
| Fred | 2 | 2 | 2 | 3 | 2 | 1 | 1 |

Scale: 5 (excellent) to 1 (beginner)

Fig. 2 Individual profiles input devices

# Location

The locations where individuals use the Internet is an indication of the physical environments where people will be seeking to employ their ICT skills. They are (Dutton and di Gennaro, 2005):

- at home;
- at work;
- someone else's home;
- educational site (e.g. school);
- public library;
- Internet cafe.

The diversity of this list indicates that learners need to be able to cope with many locations, computer setups and different facilities. This reinforces the need for learners to be able to transfer their learning and employ ICT skills and knowledge flexibly. The additional factor is the impact that portable computers such as laptops, PDAs and mobile telephones have had on the place of work. It is now common to see people working in places such as trains, in coffee bars and airport lounges. The impact of wireless technology is likely to reinforce these changes, resulting in an almost unlimited freedom to work, study or simply communicate anywhere. This will make the need for people to be independent users of ICT even more important.

# Methods

The main ways of providing education and training in user ICT skills are:

- tutor-led courses;
- drop-in centres;
- one-to-one instruction;
- self-study materials.

Tutor-led courses are probably the most traditional form of studying and are typically organised around a practical workshop environment in which each learner has an individual computer. In some cases they employ workbooks and worksheets and there is a large element of self-study. The drop-in centre is based on the concept that resources are made available so that individuals are free to attend when it is most convenient to them. This is a very worthwhile aim but does depend on the learners being sufficiently confident and skilled in learning to cope with only occasional support. One-to-one support can be provided in both traditional courses and drop-in centres as well as in the workplace when peers, supervisors and trainers can offer assistance. The success of all the approaches depends on the way the methods are employed, for example, how support is provided in a drop-in centre can be crucial. A learner who has to wait for help or who is reluctant to ask for assistance may well just drop out.

Many ICT users have learnt through trial and error, reading manuals and basically having a go. This can be effective for confident learners with a foundation of ICT skills but is often time consuming and can result in a poor coverage of skills. There are often alternative approaches to almost every ICT task, and trial and error learning can leave you with limited understanding of effective methods simply because you stumbled over a less effective alternative first when trying things out.

# Quality

The Common Inspection Framework (Ofsted and Adult Learning Inspectorate, 2001) places an emphasis on the learner by considering what they have experienced and what they expected from their course of study. This involves considering many issues such as achievements, quality of the provision, learner support, content, management, quality assurance, inclusiveness and equality of access. This demonstrates that producing high quality learning experiences is not a simple process but involves blending together many different factors.

The Common Inspection Framework provides five questions:

- How well do learners achieve?
- How effective are teaching, training and learning?
- How well do programmes and activities meet the needs and interests of learners?

- How well are learners guided and supported?
- How effective are leadership and management in raising achievement and supporting all learners?

These indicate what is expected of learning programmes and tutors. Tutors need to be able to assist learners to achieve standards and deliver learning to meet learners' needs, interests and expectations, as well as providing support and guidance. This is asking tutors to provide far more than an individual computer and a series of worksheets for the learner to progress through.

# What is ICT literacy?

There are three interrelated forms of literacy which are:

- ICT literacy;
- media literacy;
- information literacy.

These terms are often used in a way that suggests they are the same or that they substantially overlap. They clearly relate to each other but are intrinsically different. There are extensive definitions of the three forms of literacy but the sections below consider them in a straightforward way, as they may relate to teaching or training ICT users.

## ICT literacy

The ICT Skill for Life standard (QCA, 2005) is essentially the definition of the skills and knowledge required to function in a modern technological society. It considers ICT as a set of tools to help users undertake tasks and meet their needs. There is an emphasis on using ICT for purposeful activities in a wide range of contexts covering both social and economic aspects of people's lives. At Level I the intention is that learners will become independent users of ICT.

Although there is this clear emphasis on using ICT, the standard is not limited to simply the technology but has three main themes:

- working with ICT;
- finding and exchanging information;
- developing and presenting information.

These demonstrate that ICT literacy is also concerned with the use, communication and application of information created by or located through the use of ICT, showing that media and information skills are also linked to the standard.

## Media literacy

There are various definitions of media literacy. NIACE (2005a) defined it as ' ... the ability to access, analyse and respond (critically) to, and benefit from, a range of media.' Media means not simply the printed word but also all forms of electronic communication. In simple terms, people need to be able to access and employ the new forms of media such as digital television, text messaging, online discussion groups and news services. The immediate overlap with ICT skills is the need to use input and output devices in order to access digital media. This is followed by locating specific content which requires searching skills that are included in the Skill for Life standard. Finally users need to be able to make judgements of the quality of the information presented. This can prove difficult and although some aspects are covered in the Skill for Life standard, these relate mainly to information presented on websites. The full ability to analyse media extends beyond the standard. The emphasis in the NIACE definition to responding to the media again overlaps with the Skill for Life standard but probably not in sufficient depth for a fully media-literate person.

## Information literacy

The Chartered Institute of Library and Information Professionals defines information literacy by saying 'Information literacy is knowing when and why you need information, where to find it, and how to evaluate, use and communicate it in an ethical manner.' This definition suggests several different skills including:

- locating and accessing information;
- assessing the quality and suitability of the content;
- presenting and communicating the information.

Within the ICT Skill for Life standard these skills are included, although the assumption is that the information is mainly in the form of online content. However, the substantial growth in electronic forms of information makes this a major element in information literacy. A conventional library will frequently have an electronic catalogue.

ICT, media and information literacy are obviously related and overlap. When teaching or training ICT skills, it is important to realise that learning the simple mechanics of using technology is insufficient. Users need to understand factors such as judging the quality of website content. Media and information literacy are vital for the effective use of technology for social and economic benefits (Figure 3).

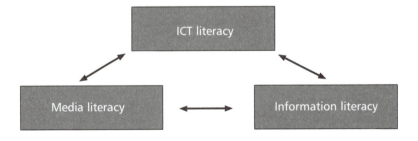

Fig. 3 Relationship between ICT, media and information literacy

# Functional and structural understanding

Many ICT programmes are almost entirely focused around helping users learn to use an application in a functional way. This can be effective as long as the learners are only using the identical application and are not required to transfer their skills to a new version or product. However, ICT is very dynamic and there is a high probability that learners will be required to use other versions or products. A functional approach in this case can leave people unable to transfer skills and baffled by the new system.

Learners need to be encouraged to identify the connections between different applications, recognise common methods and develop a more structural understanding of the technology rather than a purely functional one. The tutor has to identify opportunities arising during the course to make connections which illustrate structural issues. This places a large burden on tutors and does require that they have a wide understanding of ICT. Learners who are able to develop a degree of structural understanding will be able to transfer their learning to new applications and situations.

The analogy which is often used compares ICT user skills to driving a car, in that you do not need to know how to repair the car to use one. In a similar way it is suggested that using a computer does not require you to understand the inner workings of the technology. At a general level this is probably correct but it does help when driving a car to know, for example, when you need petrol, how often a service is required, that a particular sound probably means that the exhaust has a hole, how to top up the oil and how to change a tyre. This is essentially structural understanding and it does help a great deal when things go wrong or when changing vehicles. In a similar way, some structural knowledge of ICT is very useful when things change and in ICT they change continually.

# Self-development

ICT covers a wide and diverse range of applications, techniques and systems. It is also rapidly changing and extending so that learners who wish their skills and knowledge to remain current must continuously develop them. Employers are likely to expect that staff are motivated to maintain their professional skills through self-development. It is therefore important that users are confident in their ability to learn new skills and are able to adapt and transfer existing skills and knowledge to new situations. This will require people who are:

- self-confident;
- able to process effective learning skills;
- able to transfer their learning to new situations and applications;
- willing to explore new products and environments.

Initial and ongoing ICT user programmes need to consider how to develop people so that they have this mix of abilities and characteristics. Many adults have had poor education and training experiences which has left them with limited self-confidence and self-esteem. Several surveys of non-ICT users have revealed that many people doubt they have the ability to learn to use ICT. The National Office of Statistics (2005) reported that a third of Internet non-users had indicated that they lacked knowledge or confidence to use it. It is likely that a large proportion of learners attending an initial ICT programme will need to develop their learning skills in order for them to be able to cope with the changes that are a part of ICT.

The scale of the task is partially demonstrated by adult participation in learning. The NIACE survey of participation (Aldridge and Tuckett, 2004) reported that 38% of adults have undertaken some form of learning in the last three years. In contrast, 36% had not undertaken any form of learning since they left full-time education. The survey also identified a relationship between learning and access to the Internet, with half of all adults with Internet access also participating in learning. A third of all adults employ the Internet as part of their learning activities.

It is likely that many of the adults needing basic ICT education and training will not have taken part in previous learning programmes for several years. Their learning skills are likely to be underdeveloped and perhaps poor. They will often have limited self-confidence and self-esteem. It is important that their initial ICT experience helps them to develop other skills and attributes, and is not simply focused on ICT.

## Independent ICT users

The nature of ICT requires users who are able to constantly develop their skills, to take account both of the dynamic nature of technology with its continuous process of change and the trend towards employers requiring staff with higher levels of skill. The ICT Skill for Life standard expects learners who have achieved Level I to be independent users, but it is not entirely clear how to define this type of person. Phelphs et al (2001) provide a comprehensive analysis of a capable ICT user. Their analysis showed that the main characteristics emphasised an individual who had the capacity to develop technical skills and knowledge with an emphasis on characteristics such as confidence, persistence, a willingness to explore, a love of learning, problem-solving abilities and technical knowledge.

This description goes a long way towards defining an independent user and it is important to note that existing technical knowledge is only a part of the equation. The other characteristics are probably more important once a reasonable foundation of technical skills and knowledge is established, being based on a structural under-standing rather than a simple functional knowledge.

## Background:

# a summary of key points

—— *There is a trend for employers to want users to have more advanced ICT skills.*

—— *Learning programmes need to demonstrate that ICT is relevant to learners' lives and to provide them with confidence to learn about ICT.*

—— *ICT users need to continue to develop and extend their skills.*

—— *The level of ICT users' skills will depend on their roles and needs.*

—— *ICT users will employ their skills and knowledge in diverse locations and will become independent users.*

—— *Learning methods need to be appropriate to the user.*

—— *Tutors need to provide learning related to the achievement standards, in order to satisfy learners' needs, interests and expectations by offering appropriate support and guidance.*

—— *ICT skills and knowledge are not simply about using technology, but involve both media and information literacy.*

—— *Structural knowledge of ICT is very useful to help learners to adapt to new and changing situations.*

—— *Courses need to equip learners to cope with change by helping them to develop their learning skills.*

—— *Independent users require a range of characteristics of which technical skills are only part of the equation.*

# 2 INITIAL EXPERIENCE AND ASSESSMENT

## Introduction

The learners' initial experience of an education or training programme is crucial in that it provides a view of what to expect, confirms their decision to study and motivates them. The general aims of the first session are to:

- break the ice in helping individuals communicate with each other and with the tutor;
- explain the content of the programme;
- explain how the programme will be carried out;
- motivate the learners;
- provide them with confidence that they can learn about ICT;
- gain and direct the learners' attention to the key issues of the course;
- assess the learners' needs and experience.

It can be considered as an induction to the learning process whereby you are preparing the learners and yourself to provide a high quality experience. Some aspects may be covered earlier during information, advice and guidance activities (e.g. content, identifying learners' needs and preferred approaches) but it is useful to build on this foundation during the initial session. For adults returning to learning after an interval of several years, the initial experience is crucial to reinforce their decision to study. It is likely that simply enrolling was a substantial challenge, therefore the initial session needs to reduce their anxiety and increase their confidence.

## Breaking the ice

In any education or training programme it is important to encourage communication between the members of the group. Learners need to feel comfortable so they can ask questions and make comments. Peer support is useful in any group and needs effective communication in order to take place.

There are various different ways to start a course but effective practice is to undertake some form of introductions involving activities that are interesting and appropriate. Some options are:

- Ask each person to take a digital photograph of another member of the group and then to interview them about how they would describe themselves. This will eventually produce a poster of the class giving a picture and their names. This will help everyone to remember names and facilitate communication. The camera helps make introductions fun and encourages discussion. It also starts the initial assessment process, especially if the group is participating in a beginner's course. The way people handle the camera and discuss the process can give you some insight into their ICT experience and general confidence.

- Get each person to scan the contents of a pocket or handbag as a way of introducing themselves. It is an amusing experience and can lead to a lot of discussion as well as providing the tutor with some insight into ICT experience and confidence by observing the use of the scanner.

These approaches are inherently active. Learners are not passively listening, but are actively involved in the process. They are learning by doing useful tasks. As an initial activity this sends a message to the group that the course will be active and practical. They will also allow you to form some initial impressions of the confidence and skills of the individuals. This is not a systematic assessment but can help you to introduce a more formal initial assessment.

## Initial assessment

There are several ways of undertaking an initial assessment and they depend to a large extent on the learners. People attending their first ICT course will probably have few existing skills or understanding so that there is little point in asking them to carry out a detailed self-assessment of their ICT skills and knowledge. However, a learner taking part in an advanced level course may well have extensive ICT experience which you will need to identify to ensure that they are not asked to repeat areas they are already competent in.

Initial assessment should identify the learners' existing ICT skills and knowledge and their motives, interests and needs in taking part in the programme. This will allow you to develop an individualised learning plan for each student. There is a third area that you need to assess and this relates to the learners' previous experience of education and training. How developed are their learning and studying skills and are they confident learners? This will have a direct impact on the approaches and methods that you are able to employ (Figure 4) as well as the degree of support which they will need.

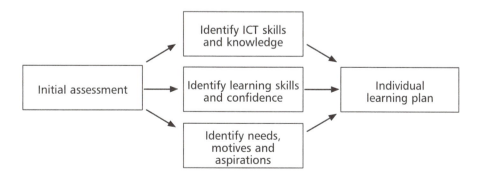

Fig. 4 Initial assessment

This can be a formidable amount of assessment to ask of learners during their first session and needs to be undertaken in a way that does not alienate them. Many people are not enthusiastic about assessment of any type and so will not be motivated if you tell them that they are going to be assessed for most of the time. However, it is perfectly possible to present assessment in a form that will be acceptable. The key is to involve the learners actively, rather than use approaches that are done to them.

## Learners' involvement

Learners should be able to play an active role in assessment. They have far more understanding of their needs, experience and expectations than anyone else. It is therefore essential that they are fully engaged in the process. Equally important is that any activity at the start of a course is likely to have a significant impact on their motivation. If they lack confidence, a poor experience may well result in their not returning. Initial assessment is an opportunity to engage with learners to demonstrate whether the course will meet their needs, be an enjoyable experience and give them confidence.

## Choosing an initial assessment product

There is a variety of assessment and diagnostic tools and systems available. Professor David Bartram (in Horsburgh and Woodlock, 2000) identified six criteria for choosing one. They are:

1. scope – what does the tool assess? Does it meet your needs?
2. validity – does it test what you need to assess?
3. reliability – who else is using the system?
4. practicality – how will the tool fit into your environment? Do you need special training to use it? How much does it cost?
5. acceptability – will the learners accept the methods employed to assess them?
6. equal opportunities – does the approach taken disadvantage some learners (e.g. people with disabilities)?

## What could be covered in initial assessment?

The information that could be identified and considered during initial assessment can be extensive. It is therefore important to realise that it should reflect the learner and that few will need all the items covered in depth. Another constraint is the nature of the learning programme so that the initial assessment is fit for purpose.

The possible areas to be covered include (DfES, 2001):

- ICT skills and knowledge;
- learners' motives, interests and needs in taking part in the programme;
- previous education and training experience (e.g. learning skills);
- skills for life (i.e. literacy, numeracy and ESOL – English for speakers of other languages);

- learning difficulties;
- support needs;
- personal circumstances;
- learning styles.

## Literacy and numeracy assessment

There are major national programmes to address the problem of the many adults with poor literacy and numeracy skills. These have developed a range of tools to help you identify adults with problems. The initial assessment pack for literacy and numeracy is available from the Basic Skills Agency. They can also provide screening tools to help you quickly identify people who may have difficulties. In addition, other suppliers, including Cambridge Training and Development and bksb (West Notting-hamshire College), have developed assessment tools.

## Dropping out

Initial assessment should also attempt to identify learners who may need more support and assistance. Learners who are returning to education or training after a long interval are often at risk of dropping out. Some will have little confidence in themselves or in their ability to develop ICT skills and knowledge. You can try to identify potential drop outs during the initial assessment. They often exhibit characteristics such as:

- lack of confidence;
- reluctance to try new equipment;
- making few contributions to discussion.

The key to preventing people from dropping out is to provide the right degree of support and to help people to realise that they can succeed. It is worthwhile trying to provide them with tasks at which they are going to succeed and to make sure they receive sufficient praise for their achievements.

# Individual learning plans

A learning plan ought to be the outcome of the initial assessment and should reflect the combined efforts of the tutor and learner. It should include details of:

- the learning objectives to be achieved;
- a timetable;
- the support needed.

It can obviously be extended far beyond this basic outline to include methods, links with other education and training programmes, work experience and assessment. The learning plans should reflect the learners' needs and the programme they are undertaking. However, in all cases it needs to be a working document, regularly reviewed at appropriate points in the course.

# Taster

One method providing a useful follow up to these opening actions is to provide a taster session in which the learners have the opportunity to try out a range of applications, communication methods and equipment. This is often used to motivate new users or to improve their confidence so that they agree to participate in a course. It is also a useful way of assessing existing skills and understanding of a range of ICT systems. A taster session might provide opportunities to:

- use a digital camera — there is a wide range of cameras and it is useful to show a variety of them (e.g. mobile phone with a built-in camera);
- use a digital sound recorder;
- use a digital video camera;
- browse the World Wide Web;
- enter text into a word processor;
- draw a picture;
- scan an image;
- look at an electronic whiteboard;
- use memory sticks;
- inspect a personal digital assistant.

An effective taster event needs several people to support the learners. It can be very engaging and motivating to learners, helping them to realise the options available, so enabling them to identify their needs and objectives for taking part in the course. The tutor should systematically talk to each learner, asking them to provide some basic information about their needs. Here are some typical questions.

- Why do you want to learn about ICT?
- What experience have you had with computers?
- Do you have access to a computer? Where? Do you know what type it is?
- What do you particularly want to learn?

Learners will often have had some experience of computers although this is often limited to observing children or friends using them. Occasionally they will have used one with the help of a friend. The DfES survey (2003) indicated that many people had a reasonable level of knowledge of ICT but very few practical skills. This can help with assessment since they may be clear about what they want to be able to do. Evidence from a variety of surveys has indicated that learners are motivated to learn about ICT in order to:

- get a job or a better job;
- develop new ICT competencies to build on existing skills;
- help their children with their education;

- fulfil social, family or simple curiosity reasons (e.g. sending e-mails to family who live overseas).

It is important to take notes and keep records of your own assessments and the comments from the learners. They will help you to develop an individual learning plan (Figure 5). This may be quite informal, aimed at helping you provide an effective learning experience or a plan that you need to agree with the individual. In either case it is the start of the individual learner record that it is useful to keep (Figure 6). These will help you track each person's progress. Figure 5 is an example of a simple layout of an individual learning plan and Figure 6 is an individual learner course record. You will need to adapt them to meet your specific circumstances.

| Title of course | | |
|---|---|---|
| Date: | Name: | Initial assessment |
| Session | Content | Comments |
| One | | |
| Two | | |
| Three | | |
| Four | | |
| Five | | |
| Six | | |
| Seven | | |
| Eight | | |

Fig. 5 Individual learning plan

Another straightforward approach to initial assessment, which can either be combined with tasters or replace them, is a checklist. This can be completed by the tutor as part of an individual conversation or by the learner, although the tutor will need to explain what each item means with ICT novices. Self-assessment is not always accurate, especially with new learners who may not fully understand the terms. Figure 7 (page 19) is an example of a simple checklist.

# Negotiated curriculum

In a typical group of a dozen adult learners you are likely to identify a wide range of needs and purposes. It is not always straightforward to plan the programme to meet these needs. You may be working within the syllabus of an ICT qualification that will limit your freedom if the aim of the course is to help everyone achieve the award. You could in theory develop 12 unique individual learning programmes but this may severely limit group or peer support since everyone will be pursuing a distinct programme. It is also likely to place enormous demands on your skills that will make this extreme very difficult to deliver.

The solution to this dilemma is to negotiate the programme with your learners. Offer them the choices of what to cover and in what order. It is likely that some learners will want to change from their initial viewpoint once they realise the full range of possibilities. It is good practice to produce a visual aid of the outcome of the negotiation so that progress can be reviewed at intervals. A negotiated approach will still leave room for individual activities, peer support and group work.

| Title of course | | |
|---|---|---|
| Start date: | Name: | |
| Finish date: | | |
| Initial assessment: | | |
| Session | Content | Notes |
| One | | |
| Two | | |
| Three | | |
| Four | | |
| Five | | |
| Six | | |
| Seven | | |
| Eight | | |
| Assessment: | | |

Fig. 6 Individual learner course record

| Information and communication checklist | | | |
|---|---|---|---|
| Item | No experience | Some experience | Competent user |
| Switching system on and off | | | |
| Using input devices | | | |
| Opening applications | | | |
| Saving files | | | |
| Opening files | | | |
| Entering text | | | |
| Editing text | | | |
| Formatting text | | | |
| Printing document | | | |

Fig. 7 Checklist

The range of documents can seem daunting, but a professional approach involves careful planning and record keeping. It is not possible to remember what many individual learners are achieving each session unless you keep records. It is vital, before you start, to understand the learners' existing skills and knowledge so that you can build on this foundation. It all involves having assessment notes, schemes of work, lesson plans and learners' records. These all form part of the evidence you need when you are inspected to demonstrate the quality of your teaching and training.

## Learning styles

It is now accepted that learners have different learning preferences or styles. This can be described in a number of ways and there are tests available to identify them. However, simple knowledge of learners' preferences on their own are not sufficient without the corresponding changes in the way that the course is presented to match them. In any group you are likely to have a range of styles, with some contradictions, so it is difficult to meet everyone's preferences all the time. The important factor is not to employ methods that are skewed in a particular direction so that some learners are seriously disadvantaged. The key is to use a mix of methods that will ensure all preferences are catered for some of the time.

Your own preferences are probably already influencing your teaching and training since your own experience of the things you like and the approaches that you have found effective will influence your own course design. The important issue is to realise that other people may well prefer a very different mix to your own.

Learning styles are often presented as a continuum, which show that although individuals like to learn through visual material they can also cope with text. Equally some learners could possibly have the opposite preferences (i.e. prefer text rather than pictures). When you are designing the programme it is important to ensure that giving information in visual and textual ways provides for both preferences. There are other aspects of learning styles which you also need to balance within the learning programmes. Some learners prefer an auditory approach whereby they hear the explanations, while others would rather touch and feel and be actively involved in the learning process.

Within the design of the programme you need to offer a range of methods so that no one is at a disadvantage and everyone's preferences are provided for some of the time. You need to combine this with the flexibility to allow learners to follow the paths they prefer. The overall mix needs to include:

- visual and textual materials;
- auditory;
- tactile;
- individual and group activities;
- practical activities and theoretical background;
- reflection and action-based tasks;
- overall context and individual components.

Figure 8 (p21) provides some examples of practical steps aligned with the learning preferences above. If you consider the actions you should notice that you can provide a balanced programme with variety and opportunities for everyone.

## Learners with disabilities

Some adults with disabilities may have difficulty using ICT. Many operating systems offer special functions to help disabled users. Microsoft Windows provides a range of accessibility options within the Control Panel. These allow you to make changes to the keyboard, mouse, sound and display to assist disabled users (Figure 9). In order to customise the system for individual learners you need to discuss the person's needs with them so that the most useful options are chosen.

It is good practice to use the option of selecting the accessibility options to demonstrate how to navigate and customise the operating system. You can work with individuals so that they gain some experience and a system that will more easily meet their needs.

| Learning preferences | Actions |
|---|---|
| Visual | 1. Use visual aids to present information<br>2. Illustrations in handouts<br>3. Use diagrams to explain concepts and content<br>4. Demonstrations |
| Text | 1. Provide handouts<br>2. Worksheets for each exercise<br>3. Produce written work |
| Auditory | 1. Explain issues through presentations<br>2. Demonstrations<br>3. Multimedia learning materials |
| Tactile | 1. Taster sessions<br>2. Practical activities<br>3. Demonstrate skills as part of assessment |
| Individual | 1. Individual exercises<br>2. Personal reviews<br>3. Individual assessment |
| Group | 1. Group exercises<br>2. Partnered exercises<br>3. Group assessment |
| Practical | 1. Worksheet exercises<br>2. Individual practical activities<br>3. Group practical activities |
| Theory | 1. Presentations to whole class<br>2. Individual coaching<br>3. Explain topics as part of assessment |
| Reflection | 1. Individual review<br>2. Group review<br>3. Learning diaries<br>4. Feedback |
| Overall context | 1. Provide overview of each new topic<br>2. Handouts covering each topic |
| Individual steps | 1. Provide step by step guidance to activities in worksheets<br>2. Demonstrate step by step |

Fig. 8 Learning preference actions

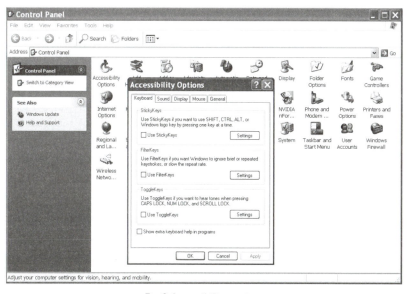

Fig. 9 Accessibility options

In addition to customising the operating system there are many other hardware and software options to modify or provide an alternative input and display devices. Some options are:

- voice input software;
- speech output systems;
- alternative input devices;
- alternative output devices.

It is useful to take specialist advice about alternative hardware and software. Ability-net offers a range of fact sheets on many useful aspects of accessibility. TechDis is a specialist service aimed at helping learners who are disabled or who have learning difficulties. They offer a wide range of resources to help accessibility including a number of guides.

NIACE has published a charter for learning for students with learning difficulties (Jacobsen, 2000) which provides a clear statement of the rights that students should be provided with. It is a powerful reminder of what you need to offer learners. It includes:

> *'Talk to us like adults.'*
>
> *'The information needs to be easy to understand.'*
>
> *'We should have a say in what we learn.'*

These statements should be considered as objectives for all your courses.

# Learning cycle

Initial assessment is not an isolated part of a course of study, but rather an integral part of the learning cycle. Figure 10 illustrates a learning cycle and is based on the DfES initial assessment good practice guide (2001). The diagram indicates that assessment is a continuous process that should be repeated at intervals to ensure that the learner's needs are being met. It requires the tutor to monitor the learner's progress so that the individual learning plan is a living document. In a similar way the learning programme needs to grow and adapt to the changing needs of the learner. This requires careful planning and a systematic approach in which you are willing to make the necessary changes based on the review of progress and the assessments undertaken.

It is useful to start each session with a brief review of the previous one, to ensure that the learners have understood the content as well as to provide them with the opportunity to ask questions and for you to assess progress. This is often a whole class activity and some individuals may be reluctant to speak in front of everyone else so it is important to provide individual opportunities to review progress. This may be informal in that you simply discuss what they are learning as you move around the group supporting their learning, or it may be formal where you consider their assignments with them. A mixture of group, individual, informal and formal is often helpful to determine an accurate picture.

The group methods may inhibit participation but have the advantage that everyone can benefit from all the comments. It is sometimes called vicarious learning and is a potential benefit of many group activities in that everyone gains from hearing the comments and questions of their peers.

Fig. 10 Learning cycle

# Balance

When you start to consider what you should ideally cover in an initial session, it can be quite daunting. If you attempt to undertake every task, the result can often be a poor session since assessment, learning cycles and learning styles will dominate at the expense of the learning experience. For many learners, simply attending a course is a challenge. Many of them will come expecting to learn about ICT which seems very reasonable. They are not likely to respond well if they spend the whole time being assessed. Most learners attending ICT programmes expect them to be highly practical and offer lots of opportunities for hands-on practice.

It is important to achieve a balance between what you need to do and the learners' expectations. Ideally you need to integrate activities such as assessment into the practical aspects of ICT such as combining tasters with assessment. Everything needs to be explained to the learners so that by the end of the session they are well informed and motivated to continue.

## Initial experience and assessment:

# a summary of key points

—— *Initial assessment should consider the whole person.*

—— *The initial experience of a course is critical in that it sets the scene for the whole programme. It is an opportunity to motivate the learners.*

—— *Tasters are often a powerful way of gaining an insight into the learners, creating a positive environment and gaining valuable evidence for assessing current skills.*

—— *In order to hold their attention and motivate them, the content of the course needs to be agreed with the learners.*

—— *Learners have distinct learning preferences (learning styles) which need to be addressed during the programme by considering the approaches and methods used.*

—— *The needs of learners with disabilities must be considered. Many applications and operating systems offer additional functions to assist some disabled learners. It is useful to take advice on best practice and to discuss individual needs with the learner.*

—— *The learning cycle provides a model to help you plan your sessions and programmes.*

—— *In the opening session consider the overall balance and put the needs of the learners first.*

# Introduction

All ICT qualifications are based on the National Occupational Standard (NOS). e-Skills UK is the ICT sector skills council and it established the National Occupational Standards for ICT. The standards are based on the needs of industry and the sector skills council represents employers. They are therefore a statement of the competencies needed by employers from across all parts of industry and commerce. The standards are regularly reviewed, since needs do change. The trend is for employers to want employees with ever increasing levels of ICT skills and knowledge. A copy of the ICT users' NOS can be downloaded from the e-skills website (*www. e-skills.com/*).

All ICT qualifications are based on the NOS. Qualifications are developed by awarding bodies but they must be approved by the Qualifications and Curriculum Authority (QCA). You can find a list of all QCA approved qualifications at *www.openquals.org.uk*. This site provides a search facility to locate any approved qualification on the QCA database. The database will provide information about the period of approval for the qualification since changes to the NOS will result in amendments to the qualifications. All qualifications are only approved for specific periods of time.

The awarding bodies which develop the qualifications can provide detailed guidance about the nature of the award. This often takes the form of:

- mandatory and optional units;
- assessment criteria;
- details of content of units;
- examples of assessment tests.

To deliver a specific qualification your centre normally needs to be accredited by the awarding body. The process varies but again information on the procedure is available from the individual awarding body. Approved centres are kept informed of developments relating to the qualification and this will often include briefings when it is revised.

# ICT Skill for Life

In 2003, the White Paper '21st Century Skills Realising Our Potential' acknowledged that ICT was a new Skill for Life. This means that ICT is an essential set of skills and knowledge for a citizen of Great Britain in the twenty-first century. ICT joined literacy, numeracy and English for speakers of other languages (ESOL) as a Skill for Life. In order to specify what specific skills were required for ICT Skills for Life,

QCA developed a set of standards covering Entry Level I to Level 2. These are available from the QCA website (*www.qca.gov.uk*). These are effectively a subset of the National Occupational Standards and define the minimum standard for an ICT user in order to function in a modern society. The standard comes with a series of examples of purposeful use of ICT since it is intended to be delivered in a purposeful way, that is, in a way that is relevant to and meets the needs of learners.

All Skills for Life also have a core curriculum. The ICT Core Curriculum (2005) is available from the QCA website or as a publication from the Department for Education and Skills. The Curriculum document provides:

- explanation of the standard in terms of specific skills and knowledge the learners need to achieve;
- examples of the skills, knowledge and understanding required;
- guidance on teaching and learning ICT Skills for Life;
- scenarios – examples of learners' activities in relation to the curriculum;
- guidance on the definition of each level.

If you are teaching ICT as a Skill for Life it is essential to have a copy of the curriculum. Awarding bodies have received approval for qualifications that meet the Skill for Life standards.

A key difference between ICT Skill for Life standards and more traditional ICT qualifications is purpose, in that learners are expected to learn and be taught in a purposeful way. This means that their needs and aspirations must be identified and the course activities aimed to meet them. Learners who want to improve their ICT skills in order to work in an office are likely to need to develop skills such as word processing, using spreadsheets, finding information on the World Wide Web and communicating with e-mail. Alternatively older learners who are seeking to use the World Wide Web to help them trace their family history may need an emphasis on search techniques, judging the quality of information and e-mail communication. The ICT Skill for Life standard is independent of specific applications and is focused on using computers and finding and presenting information allowing for a range of alternative applications to be used.

## ICT Skill for Life National Curriculum

The ICT Skill for Life standards were converted into a national curriculum following the pattern established for literacy, numeracy and English for speakers of other languages. The curriculum document provides an overview of the standards considering the key issues of purposeful learning, definitions of levels, assessment and relationships with key skills and the other Skills for Life. The main body of the document systematically considers the delivery of the standard by providing the standard alongside a statement of what the learners must achieve, with examples of the knowledge, skills and understanding associated with achieving it and finally suggestions for teachers linked to the specific part of the standards. At the end of the document is a range of scenarios giving examples of the ICT Skill for Life being delivered in particular contexts.

The curriculum document is essential if you are delivering ICT Skill for Life but it also offers a great deal of useful advice and suggestions for anyone helping new ICT users become competent.

# Embedding ICT within other subjects

ICT is often employed to deliver and support learning (i.e. e-learning) and it is clear that by using technology in this way many learners gain the additional bonus of some improved or new ICT skills and knowledge. This has led to the possibility of integrating ICT within another subject so that learners achieve two outcomes. These ideas are particularly associated with the other Skills for Life since ICT has been used extensively to support learners developing their literacy, numeracy and language skills.

The ICT Action research project (NIACE, 2005b) considered the possibility of embedding or integrating ICT with the other Skills for Life as one aspect of the research. The project showed that there was a clear potential to achieve the double outcome although there was a variety of practical issues, including the need for tutors with dual skills and knowledge of the two subjects, mapping the two standards against each other and a careful consideration of how to link them.

## Example

*Assisting the development of writing skills through word processing: the word processor allows learners to revise, edit and produce high quality and motivating documents. A hand written document would take far longer to revise since it would involve writing the entire piece again, whereas a word processor allows you to concentrate on the areas you are seeking to improve.*

Clarke (2006) has considered the integration of ICT with the financial literacy framework. This provides the standard for people seeking to become financially literate. ICT has been used as the means of supporting the development of financial skills and knowledge through initiatives such as Money Matters To Me, a website offering resources to assist the delivery of financial education. Clarke has mapped the ICT Skill for Life standard against the financial literacy framework and suggests many learning activities linking the two subjects.

## Example

*Using a spreadsheet to develop a family budget plan: the continuing growth in the use of e-learning enhances the possibilities of embedding ICT within many different subjects. However, to successfully achieve the desired double outcome requires a significant amount of preparation and planning, not least the systematic mapping of the different standards in relation to each other and a careful consideration of learning activities.*

# Key Skills

Key Skills are aimed principally at young people so that they are equipped for the workplace, society and education by having a foundation in a range of skills. At the moment key skills cover:

- the application of number;
- communication;
- ICT;
- improving own learning and performance;
- problem-solving;
- working with others.

Each Key Skill has an accompanying standard, available from the Qualifications and Curriculum Authority (QCA) website, which defines the skills at Levels 1 to 4. Key Skills and Skills for Life will eventually be replaced by a single set of functional skills.

## Basic skills

The term 'basic skills' is still widely used but they are now known as Skills for Life. Basic skills applies to literacy and numeracy while Skills for Life include literacy, numeracy, ESOL and ICT. The Basic Skills Agency can offer assistance and information about Skills for Life (i.e. literacy and numeracy).

# Qualifications Framework

The National Qualifications Framework for England, Wales and Northern Ireland provides an overall structure of levels that allow qualifications to be compared and learners to plan their education. The framework was revised in 2004 and increased the number of Levels from 6 to 9. The original Entry Level to Level 3 was not altered so the area associated with ICT User qualifications has not been changed. Figure 11 shows a comparison of the original levels with both the revised ones and higher education and other qualifications. It is based on the diagram on the QCA website (Structure of the NQF). Although the table may indicate equivalents, there are likely to be significant differences in qualifications across the table rows.

| Framework | | Higher education or other qualifications |
| --- | --- | --- |
| Original levels | New levels | |
| Level 5 | Level 8 | Doctorate (PhD) |
| | Level 7 | Masters Degree |
| Level 4 | Level 6 | Honours Degree |
| | Level 5 | Higher Education Diploma |
| | Level 4 | Higher Education Certificate |
| Level 3 | Level 3 | Advanced GCSE |
| Level 2 | Level 2 | GCSE |
| Level 1 | Level 1 | No equivalent |
| Entry Levels 1 to 3 | Entry Levels 1 to 3 | No equivalent |

Fig. 11 National Qualifications Framework

# National Vocational Qualifications

National Vocational Qualifications (NVQs) began in the 1980s and are based on occupational competency. They are designed to test the competency of individuals carrying out specific occupations. They are linked to the National Occupation Standards in each occupational area (e.g. retail) and should be able to inform an employer that the holder of a NVQ is competent in a defined range of tasks, that they have the skills and knowledge to undertake the tasks. The learners demonstrate their skills and knowledge in the workplace by successfully carrying out the task as part of the NVQ assessment, proving their competency by providing evidence such as:

- witness statements;
- outcomes of the task;
- photographs.

The NVQs define both what is acceptable as evidence and how it must be presented. This is often in the form of a portfolio of evidence which is normally mapped against the list of competencies that the qualification requires of the individual. The competencies are defined in context by being accompanied by performance criteria and range statements that show how the competency needs to be demonstrated. A competence statement may be broken down into elements of competence with accompanying performance criteria and range statement.

## Information Technology Qualification

The NVQ for ICT is called the ITQ (Information Technology Qualification) and is available at Levels 1, 2 and 3. It has been designed to be a flexible qualification in order to meet the different needs of ICT users in all organisational contexts. It consists of a core unit which is compulsory and a range of optional units. This enables learners and employers to select the mixture that is most appropriate to their needs.

The ITQ allows you to select units at different levels so that you can include Level 2 units in a Level 3 award or Level 1 units in a Level 2 award. There are conditions about what you can combine to gain the qualification and the minimum amount of the higher-level contribution that needs to be incorporated in the qualification.

This flexibility allows the award to be customised for different roles in different types of enterprises. There are significant differences between the ICT skills and knowledge that users need in different occupations.

## Example

- *Manager – emphasis on communication technologies, spreadsheets and word processing.*
- *Sales staff – emphasis on presentation applications, databases and spreadsheets.*

*There are also likely to be differences in levels of skills needed.*

There is considerable interest in using ITQ for teachers and trainers in two particular areas:

- ICT skills and knowledge so that the teacher or trainer could employ e-learning methods and applications;
- ICT skills and knowledge needed to deliver the ICT Skill for Life – this involves both ICT specialist practitioners and other Skills for Life teachers.

In terms of e-learning, the mix of ICT skills and knowledge will vary with the subject being taught and the e-learning approach being employed.

## Example

1. **History – searching for relevant information on the World Wide Web, judging the quality of sources and the design of learning resources.**
2. **Floristry – using digital cameras, editing applications and using storage systems as a means of providing evidence for learners' evidence portfolios.**
3. **Dance – video cameras so that they can be used as a means of providing effective feedback on the learners' practical skills.**

**The ITQ could provide a means of dealing with these differences.**

Appendix 2 (page 119) illustrates four example profiles of ICT tutors who may teach the ICT Skill for Life curriculum.

1. Tutor who is working in an environment with technical support and helping learners develop their skills to Level 2.

2. Tutor who is working in an environment with technical support and helping learners develop their skills to Entry Level.

3. Tutor who is working in the community without technical support and helping learners develop their skills to Level 2.

4. Tutor who is working in the community without technical support and helping learners develop their skills to Entry Level.

The ITQ is accompanied by the e-skills passport which enables individuals to assess their own skills and knowledge and employers to define the profile of ICT skills they require of employees.

## Functional Skills

In the 14-19 Education and Skills Reform White Paper and the Skills White Paper, March 2005, the government announced functional skills. The government's policy is to define the fundamental or core aspects of English, Mathematics and ICT as Functional Skills. These are the skills which an individual needs in order to be able to live their lives confidently, effectively and independently in a modern society. The functional skills will bring together key skills, skills for life, National Curriculum and occupational standards.

Functional skills will cover both children and adults and will have a set of qualifications covering them, but in addition will underpin GCSEs in the relevant subjects. The standards for functional skills are being developed by the Qualifications and Curriculum Agency on behalf of the Department for Education and Skills.

## Standards:

# a summary of key points

— **ICT Skill for Life – ICT has been identified by the government as a fundamental skill to enable people to play a full part in modern society in a similar way to those of literacy and numeracy.**

— **ICT Skill for Life National Curriculum has been developed by QCA to assist tutors and trainers to delivery the ICT Skill for Life standard.**

— **Embedding ICT within other subjects has considerable potential, in that ICT is often employed as e-learning in the support and delivery of learning. This offers the opportunity to develop ICT skills alongside another subject.**

— **The National Qualifications Framework provides an overall structure of levels that allow qualifications to be compared and learners to plan their education.**

— **National Vocational Qualifications (NVQs) are based on occupational competency. They are designed to test the competency of individuals carrying out specific occupations. They are linked to the National Occupation Standards in each occupational area.**

— **The ITQ is the NVQ for ICT. It is a flexible qualification available at levels 1 to 3 and allows learners to include units from different levels in their overall award. It is linked to the e-skills passport to allow learners to self-assess.**

— **Functional skills are being developed for both young people and adults to replace key skills and skills for life. They will cover English, mathematics and ICT.**

## Introduction

Gagne (1977) provided a systematic structure for planning instruction.

1. Motivate the learners.
2. Explain the objectives of the learning programme.
3. Gain and direct learners' attention.
4. Encourage learners to consider their previous experience.
5. Offer learners help in identifying the key learning points.
6. Assist learners to retain their learning.
7. Help learners to transfer their learning.
8. Provide learners with feedback on their performance.

This structure can be used to consider the whole programme or individual learning objectives. The first session of a programme might concentrate on explaining the overall objectives of the course, and assessing the learners' current skills and knowledge, combined with identifying their reasons for attending. This would assist with points 1, 2 and 4. During the preparation of a worksheet, the tutor could present the key learning points and offer an exercise relating to the learners' interests. This would contribute 1, 3 and 5 while the later acts of marking the work would offer opportunities for feedback and retention (i.e. points 6 and 8). The framework offers a way of planning and managing your programmes. It has the advantage of offering you a structured approach to learning, but there is the danger that it may reduce flexibility if not applied sensitively within your own context.

## Motivation

Adult learners come to learning with a lifetime of experience which offers many opportunities to provide purposeful learning. They often have aims and expectations of what ICT can do for them. These may be combined with limited confidence of both ICT and their ability to learn. This will often hinder identifying their motivation to attend if you simply ask them, but this should not stop you doing so. It is important to provide a relaxing, friendly and non-threatening environment in which they can explain. There is a wide variety of ways of starting a course but some examples are:

- ask the students to introduce themselves and say why they are attending;
- divide groups into pairs and ask them to prepare to introduce their partners to the whole group;

- divide into small groups and ask them to list why people want to learn about ICT and then to identify their individual reasons among the list;

- ask each person to take a digital photograph of another member of the group and create a group poster with each person's name. This will help everyone remember the names of their group members;

- offer the opportunity to try out a range of technologies so that you are able to undertake a basic assessment of their existing knowledge and skills, but also to discuss with them their interests in ICT.

All these activities are intended to be interesting and motivating. They should help you to understand the learners' reasons for attending so that you can provide relevant experiences. Motivation is critical to the success of any learning programme. It is essential to identify positive outcomes and progress. In the initial session learners need to believe that their expectations are going to be met, that the human environment will be suitable and that they will not be made to look foolish.

The physical layout of an ICT workshop is often unhelpful in layout in that learners will often be placed with their backs to each other and you need to counter its effects by encouraging peer support and group activity. A central table or asking learners to form a circle can assist when you need to discuss issues away from the computers.

## Objectives

Learners will often have read marketing information about a course before registration, but it is still critical to explain what the programme aims to achieve during the sessions. This is best done in terms of what the learners will be able to do with their skills, using language that they will understand. It is poor practice only to say that they will achieve a specific qualification. Many learners will not know the syllabus and even if they do, it may well be written in terms of ICT skills.

### Example

- *Ability to enter text into a word-processor – this would be better expressed as ability to write a letter.*

- *Achieve a level 2 qualification – this would be better expressed as a qualification that will provide you with the skills you will need to gain a job.*

There are many opportunities for you to explain the objectives for the course or a specific exercise, including:

- start of each session – this week we will … ;

- introduction to an exercise – by the end of the assignment you will be able to … ;

- reviewing – you are now able to … ;

- ask learners to identify what they have learnt and compare that to the objectives of the course.

The possibility of achieving a qualification will motivate some learners, but is also likely to worry others. Poor previous experience of education will often remain with people for decades, so that you need to approach the assessment process of any course with care. In either case, the objectives of the assessment need to be presented in the learners' own terms.

## Attention

A key role of any tutor is to gain and direct the learners' attention to important points. Adults are used to making decisions about themselves. They are self-directed so that they can make choices if allowed to do so. However, it is important that these choices are based on the learners being well informed. Obviously the overall structure of the course is designed to direct the learners' attention to the important points, but a tutor needs to take advantage of each part of the learners' experience.

## Example

*Select each exercise to illustrate important issues.*

*Make links between each element of the course and the learners' individual objectives.*

*Demonstrate to individuals, groups and the whole class to gain their attention.*

*Ask learners to turn away from their computers so that they are not distracted when you are explaining a topic.*

It is important to provide the learning in the context appropriate to the learner (e.g. these skills are required by many employers; this can help your children's learning and this can help you manage your collection).

## Experience

Learners will judge new learning against their existing understanding. They will seek to make links between the new experience and their existing knowledge. If they find that it does not fit, then they are likely to be confused and find mastering the new material difficult. In ICT you can see this in many ways. Learners who have learnt on a laptop using a touch pad or similar device will often find switching to a mouse a challenge. The reverse is also true. The small differences between two different systems can be a source of confusion, while the realisation that there are similarities is a key aid to learning.

Tutors need to demonstrate the relationships between new knowledge and skills and existing ones, or provide ways for the learners to establish the relationships for themselves. There are many ways of providing a link to learners' previous experiences such as:

- designing exercises so that they are relevant to the learners (e.g. use the Internet to plan a business trip for sales staff, find information about unemployment benefits for a worker recently made redundant, and design a leaflet for members of a community organisation);

- asking learners to bring activities that they need to be able to undertake from home or work;

- creating exercises and activities that build on previous experiences (e.g. taking a digital photograph is followed by editing the image using cropping tools);

- assessing learners' existing skills and providing exercises that extend these skills and this knowledge.

# Guidance

Learners need to be guided to see the links between each part of their studies, to recognise that there are relationships between different aspects. For new learners it is important that they are guided to realise that these relationships exist. Some examples are:

- Application functions only operate if the aspect that they are working on is identified. This is achieved by highlighting the object (e.g. highlight a word to be copied).

- Hyperlinks are shown by underlining words.

- Functions change with context so if you highlight a file then the associated menus change the options they offer (e.g. rename the file).

Diagrams and images are often a useful way of illustrating relationships. To explain a hyperlink to a new Internet user in words can be difficult, but an illustration will often help and a demonstration will complete the picture.

Each learner's mistake or success is an opportunity to reinforce the learning and to show the relationships. It can also be used as an example to assist the whole group. It is important to realise that an answer to a question that everyone can hear is helpful to the whole group. Consider how often it occurs to you, when hearing a question, that you intended to ask something similar. In a group you will have the benefit of hearing the answers.

# Retention

The retention of learning is clearly an important part of the learning process. There is little point in learners who are unable to employ their skills as soon as the course is completed. The aim should be to retain understanding for as long as possible. Retention can be assisted by:

- practice – learners are able to practise their new skills.

- structure – learners are provided with a structure or framework showing how the new skills and knowledge relate to their existing understanding.

It is therefore important that the course allows the learners to try out their new skills and knowledge while linking their developing understanding to their existing knowledge. This will help them to recall and retain their learning.

The other form of retention refers to minimising drop outs from the course. Sadler and Smith (2004) identify a range of factors that influence drop outs. They include:

- helping learners to choose the right course for themselves;
- initial assessment so that the learners receive appropriate support;
- identifying learners most likely to drop out so that they can be given help;
- customising learning materials of all types to make it easy to understand;
- motivating students (e.g. showing them they are making progress);
- support (e.g. providing adequate and appropriate assistance);
- peers (e.g. support from other learners is often effective).

Many of these points are also valuable parts of planning an effective programme and we will discuss them in other parts of the book.

## Transfer

A critical risk in teaching ICT skills is that the learners fail to understand how they can transfer their understanding to new situations. In order to achieve the ability to transfer, learners need to gain experience of using their skills and understanding in new contexts. They need the opportunity to practise in a variety of contexts so they develop their ability to transfer. ICT can provide many contexts so once learners know how to save a file in a word processor, they can have the opportunity to save a file in other applications. They should be able to see the things in common between the different contexts and thus develop an understanding that can enable them to cope with other situations in which files are saved.

It is important that the course provides opportunities to transfer understanding to new situations and allows learners to be made aware of when they succeed. Some possible examples are:

- saving files in a range of applications;
- cutting, pasting and copying in and between applications;
- undertaking a task using different approaches (e.g. create a table in a word processor, database and a spreadsheet);
- managing files created by a variety of applications;
- locating files stored on different medium (e.g. hard drives, CD-ROMs, memory sticks, servers and floppy disks).

## Feedback

Feedback is a critical factor in any learning programme and should feature as a regular component of each session. It is essentially continuous in that you should be giving encouragement, correcting misconceptions and providing assessments. There are many opportunities to provide feedback to the individual learner or the whole group. You could:

- offer comments as you move around the room observing each learner's progress (this is also an opportunity to receive feedback from individuals and to judge if the explanation given or the learning materials provided are adequate);
- start each session with a brief overview of the previous one, thereby allowing you to offer help;
- review individual progress at regular intervals (e.g. on completion of each assignment);
- ask each group to comment on the exercises undertaken (this offers the tutor an opportunity to provide specific feedback combined with general feedback to the whole group);
- provide an opportunity for questions to be asked at the end of a session (this allows feedback to be given in a way that gives everyone the benefit of hearing the answers).

A few words of encouragement and support at the right time can be a powerful motivator. Motivation is critical. Adult learners will give far more to an activity if they can perceive an outcome of value to themselves. It is important to use feedback to demonstrate the relevance of a task. There are many ways of doing this such as by showing them an appropriate context, helping them solve a problem or demonstrating the usefulness and practicality of an exercise. Many learners need assistance to realise how an application could be relevant to them.

## Environment

Learners are influenced by their surroundings so it is important to provide a suitable environment that will create the right attitude to learning. The ICT room should be:

- suitable for teaching and learning;
- fit for purpose in that it helps individuals to learn about ICT;
- motivating to the learners.

In order to develop the right atmosphere you need to consider what you are aiming to do. What activities will the learners undertake in the room? What physical resources will you need? How much space will be needed? What equipment is required?

In most cases you will have a room provided that has a fixed layout since computers are not easy to move around unless you are employing portable equipment in a community or other location. In that case you have more freedom but probably less suitable facilities (e.g. insufficient power points or only a single Internet link). There is always a compromise to be reached but it is important to consider all the available space that you can use. The computer room may be limited, but perhaps you can use waiting areas or canteen facilities for small group discussions or preparatory work.

Figure 12 shows four layouts that you may encounter. The layouts are:

- **Top left hand corner** The computer systems are arranged around the walls so that the learners have their backs to the centre of the room. The tutor can walk around the room, observe progress and offer help. The main limitation is that it is difficult to gain the attention of the whole group unless they have swivel chairs, combined with clear directions when they need to turn round. Learners are side by side so it is relatively straightforward to encourage peer support.

- **Top right hand corner** This is a stereotypical classroom layout with computer systems arranged in rows. This may give the impression to adult learners that they have returned to school and that the course is teacher-centred since they all face the tutor at the front. This layout makes it difficult to observe the work of each learner and offer them appropriate support. It is easy to gain the attention of the whole group and, because learners are sitting next to each other, peer support is possible. However, due to the classroom layout, learners may be discouraged from talking to each other.

- **Bottom left hand corner** This layout clusters learners into small groups, so encouraging mutual support and making group work more straightforward. The tutor is free to walk around, observe and offer individual support. This is an effective layout if you have several groups of learners working at different speeds. However, it does require the tutor to identify similar learners. There is a problem gaining the attention of the whole class, but usually this is not too difficult since most rooms have a natural front.

- **Bottom right hand corner** This is a variation of the top left layout with the addition of some tables in the centre of the room. This allows learners to form groups, come together for whole class activities and discuss issues.

Each of the layouts has a mixture of strengths and weaknesses and you need to decide on what you are aiming to achieve or how to overcome the limitations of a room where you are unable to change the layout.

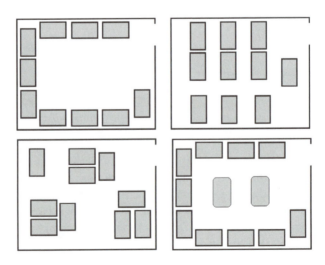

Fig. 12 Room layouts

The physical characteristics of a room such as acoustics, visibility, light and heat are important. The tutor needs to check the room by:

- sitting in each seat and gauging the visibility; can everyone see the slides, whiteboard or other visual aids?
- checking the sound levels with all the computers switched on;
- examining the lights to ensure that monitors do not reflect them and glare;
- checking the temperature with all the computers working since they will all generate heat which may be pleasant in winter yet overwhelming in summer.

There are limitations to what a tutor can achieve, but at least windows can be opened or closed, radiators switched off or lights dimmed. Consult the group, since one person's hot room is another's just-right temperature.

# Classroom management

There is a balance to be achieved between preparation and flexibility. You want to ensure that you are well prepared to offer excellent learning opportunities while also being able to respond to the needs of the learners. Planning a session is essential, but insisting on carrying out the plan when the group indicates that they need to cover other material is poor. The tutor needs to establish a balance.

A lively, buoyant group is important as an aid to learning, but a chaotic process will not help anyone. It is important to plan to maximise learning. There are many things to consider such as the following:

## Workshop organisation

There is a need to establish a balance between approaches such as:

- individual exercises;
- pairs;
- small groups;
- whole class.

It is unlikely that any one method will be suitable in all situations.

## Support

- Tutor – how much support can you personally provide?
- Support staff – how to employ them to maximise benefits?
- Peer support – how to apply and encourage most effectively?

Other staff or volunteer helpers need to be briefed so that they understand their role.

## Planning

These items interrelate and you need to plan how to integrate them:

- identify outcomes of the learning programme;
- identify appropriate teaching and learning techniques;
- create materials (e.g. exercises, handouts and worksheets).

Managing the learning process:

- plan and structure learning activities;
- identify appropriate teaching and learning techniques;
- communicate effectively with learners;
- promote and encourage individual learning;
- consider pace of learning in relation to learners.

## Reviewing the learning process with learners

Select and develop resources to support learning:

- identify assignment or activities that learners could undertake between formal sessions;
- facilitate the learning of groups;
- facilitate the learning through experience;
- establish and maintain and effective learning environment;
- identify the required outcomes of learning programmes.

Evaluation of learning materials:

- locate materials;
- judge their suitability.

## Observation

It is important to be aware of the importance of observing learners, so check the whole environment systematically to ensure you are able to gain a clear view of each learner.

# Session plans and schemes of work

Figure 13 shows an example of a session plan while Figure 14 illustrates part of a scheme of work. Both demonstrate ways that will help you plan and manage a learning programme. A session plan concentrates on an individual session and will normally consider the learning objectives you are aiming to help the learners achieve alongside the activities you are going to include. It should include approximate timings, with a note of the resources that you will need and often the context of the session (e.g. qualification being studied).

The scheme of work is based on a fictional course aimed at helping learners to use spreadsheets, and is intended to show the aims and objectives, content and approach to be taken. It may cover a whole programme, a specific theme or themes. It can be considered as a series of learning activities or events which will assist the learner to master the topic. There is a variety of ways to develop a scheme of work but some general suggestions are:

- work from the most straightforward to the most complex;
- consider what the learner already understands and start there;
- identify key sections;
- identify links to other themes.

Both plans and schemes are aimed at encouraging a systematic approach to preparing for the course and each session. They ensure that every item is considered and no aspect is neglected.

---

**Session plan**

**Title**:   Introduction to Computers for Parents

**Course**: New CLAIT (2006)

**Time and duration**:   7pm to 9pm Tuesday

**Session**:        One

**Aims and objectives**:

> By the end of the session the learners will be able to:
>
> 1. Explain their main motivation for attending an ICT course
>
> 2. Identify the main computer constituent parts
>
> 3. Use keyboard and mouse to undertake basic interaction with system

**Activities and timings**:

> 1. Introductions/initial assessment (30 minutes)
>
> 2. Taster/initial assessment (45 minutes)
>
> 3. Input device exercise (35 minutes)
>
> 4. Review of session (10 minutes)

Resources:        New CLAIT Level One, Alan Clarke, Hodder and Stoughton

Qualification:    New CLAIT (revised 2006)

---

Fig. 13 Session plans

| Session | Aims and objectives | Content | Learning approach |
|---|---|---|---|
| 1 | Familiarisation with Spreadsheet | Welcome and introduction<br><br>Enter simple sheet to identify cells, rows and columns | Introductions in pairs<br><br>Demonstration of spreadsheet<br><br>Individual exercise |
| 2 | Use functions to total rows and columns<br><br>Replication of functions | Using initial exercise to practise creating totals and replication | |
| 3 | | | |
| 4 | | | |
| 5 | | | |
| 6 | | | |
| 7 | | | |

Fig. 14 Scheme of work (spreadsheets)

# Observation

Observation is often used as a continuous professional development method whereby a colleague or manager watches your performance and provides feedback. However, there is another application of observation which is managing your classroom. In a typical computer workshop learners will be concentrating on the display in front of them and with their backs to the tutor. This is not ideal for observing what they are doing, but if you move around the room you gain the advantage of different angles so can frequently obtain a clear view. This allows you to identify learners who have problems (e.g. not interacting with the system, repeating actions over and over again and struggling to complete the exercise).

Observation will usually need to be confirmed by a question or two but it will often indicate where you need to make an effort. This is not only for remedial work but to identify quick learners who need a new stimulus so that they can work at their own faster pace. The key is to move around the workshop and watch what is happening. The view from a desk at the front is often very limited.

# Evaluating resources

An important aspect of planning any programme, course or session is to consider the resources that you will need. In some cases you will have to create them yourself but there is a wide range of ICT learning resources available. These can be professionally published materials from educational publishers, colleagues' materials and content that is freely available (e.g. on the World Wide Web). To select the most useful content you need to evaluate them. These resources are often very important to the success of the course, so it is worth investing effort in checking their suitability.

There is a variety of ways of evaluating content. Some useful questions and ideas are:

- source – who produced the materials (e.g. publisher, government agency or an educational provider)?

- are they endorsed by an appropriate organisation (e.g. awarding body)?

- appearance – size, colour and illustrations – it is important that they are attractive and motivating. You need to consider how the learners will use the publication (e.g. hold them, lay them down beside their computer or read from the monitor).

- content – does it cover the whole syllabus or only part of it? There is a considerable difference in price if a publication covers all the content or only one unit in a five-unit course.

- resources – how many exercises does the publication provide? What range of contexts is included (e.g. work, home, leisure and family)?

- extra resources – are additional resources provided (e.g. CD-ROM of exercise or a website)?

- feedback – comments from colleagues and reviews can help you to pick the most appropriate.

- learning styles – consider how the resource will meet different learners' preferences. You will often need alternatives so that learners are not disadvantaged.

You might choose to consider how the resource approaches the most difficult aspect of a course. If this is well done it may indicate a quality resource. That said, probably the most effective approach is to ask a group of learners for their views. It is always useful to ask for feedback at the end of a programme about the materials used.

## Planning and managing:

# a summary of key points

_____ *Gagne offers an approach to planning a programme.*

_____ *The main aspects to consider are: motivation, learning objectives, attention, previous experience, identification of the key learning points, retention of learning, transfer of learning and feedback.*

_____ *The environment is a key factor in creating an effective climate for learning.*

_____ *Session plans and schemes of work offer you the means to prepare carefully for your course.*

_____ *Time spent evaluating resources to identify the most suitable is never wasted.*

## 5 CONTEXT

## Introduction

There are a number of reasons why an individual may want to learn about ICT and, in a similar way, a wide range of environments in which to use technology. The Skill for Life standard offers five contexts for the use of ICT. These cover most of the areas that people are likely to be interested in, although learners will often have a range of interests, so be careful not to stereotype them. They are:

- citizen and community;
- economic activity;
- domestic and everyday life;
- leisure;
- education and training.

When teaching or training people to use ICT it is important to understand their needs and the environments in which they want to employ their skills. This will motivate them, especially if activities can be provided to meet their needs, since they will be undertaking purposeful action.

It is good practice to ask learners to bring examples of tasks that interest them and to build activities around these practical examples. Over time you will gather a wide range of materials, ideas and activities which will be a major asset in preparing your programmes.

## Citizen and community

Government services are increasingly available online. You can e-mail your Member of Parliament, submit your income tax return, tax your car online and simply discover information about a vast range of public activities through the World Wide Web. Without access to the Internet and the skills to use it, people are unable to benefit from the ease of communication and information that ICT provides in order to participate as a citizen. In addition local communities and organisations are employing technology in a vast range of imaginative ways to facilitate their activities. The list of examples below is far from exhaustive but may serve to illustrate possible ways of providing context in this area.

## Examples

1. **Visit the 10 Downing Street website and discover the history of the building.**
2. **Visit the Public Records Office website and discover how to gain access to their information about your father's army records.**
3. **Identify the local council website and discover what services your council tax pays for. This provides opportunities for discussion about access to public information and the danger of excluding people from knowledge about how government works. It could also be used as part of financial education and in understanding how council tax is calculated.**
4. **Design a community newsletter that would engage people in local activities.**
5. **Search for information about government priorities. This allows learners to practise searching skills, and also assess the quality and relevance of the information discovered.**
6. **Send an e-mail to your Member of Parliament or local councillor about an issue that concerns you.**
7. **Create a community group website (e.g. gardening club, Women's Institute, village band or youth club).**
8. **Maintain records of a community organisation's membership (e.g. subscriptions paid).**
9. **Send an e-mail with information attachment about the Neighbourhood Watch to all the group members.**
10. **Publish a book about the community, using desktop publishing or as a webpage or downloadable file.**

Often when we discuss communities we mean a geographical area, but online communication supports the development of communities of interest, which are not limited by location. Members can be anywhere in the world. The interest can relate to almost any subject. In order to be an active member of an online community, an individual needs to be able to communicate effectively through a range of methods.

- **E-mail** – sending, responding, using attachments, netiquette and managing messages.

- **Mailgroups** – these are grouped so that when you send an e-mail to one address it is copied to all the members. This allows a group discussion to take place about relevant topics.

- **Bulletin boards** – this is essentially an online location at which you can post messages for other people who use the location. It is different from a mailgroup in that you need to access the site to read the messages whereas mailgroups send them to you.

- **Learning platforms** – this is an online space in which a range of services is located, such as learning resources, mailgroups and bulletin boards. They were originally aimed at large educational institutions such as universities, but some open source ones are now available and are starting to be used by community organisations.

- **Text conferencing** – this is a way of having a synchronous group discussion through the use of text messages.

These technologies and others offer the possibility of developing online communities. There is also nothing to prevent a geographical community benefiting from online communication.

# Economic activity

Information and communication technology has changed, and is still changing, the world of work. It is now a significant part of almost all jobs. If you order food in a restaurant, your order is often transmitted to the kitchen electronically, managers are able to stay in touch with their offices through hand-held e-mail devices, delivery routes can be planned online and there are many other examples of the impact of technology on work practices.

For many learners employment is a major part of their lives and often a significant reason behind wanting to improve their ICT skills and knowledge. The employment could be paid or unpaid. This obviously covers a very wide range of roles and responsibilities. The use of ICT in the workplace is complex, covering many different tasks.

## Examples

1. *Word processing documents of all types (e.g. minutes of meetings, business letters and internal memos).*
2. *Mail merging – sending a standard letter to all the enterprise's customers about a new product.*
3. *Spreadsheets to analyse a wide variety of numerical information (e.g. project budgets, survey results and models of staff sickness).*
4. *Entering information into an organisation's customer contacts databases.*
5. *Searching for information in product databases.*
6. *Recording meetings through digital sound recordings so that accurate minutes can be produced.*
7. *Locating information on the organisation's Intranet (e.g. expense claim forms, details of staff and company business plans).*
8. *Seeking information on the World Wide Web (e.g. rail timetables, government white papers and product information).*
9. *Booking rail and airline tickets online.*
10. *Purchasing products online.*
11. *Designing web pages so that they can be kept up to date.*
12. *Creating electronic documents for downloading from the website.*
13. *Communicating with colleagues using e-mail, text messages and mobile phones.*
14. *Organising individuals with electronic diaries.*
15. *Preparing sales presentations.*

ICT is also vital in all types of employment, self-employment and unpaid work. The list of examples below is far from exhaustive but may serve to illustrate possible ways of providing context in this area. There is also considerable overlap between all the forms of employment. A large commercial organisation, a sole trader and a voluntary body all need to keep records, communicate with suppliers and customers, and market their services. The difference is often one of the scale and available resources. A self-employed person working on their own can still significantly improve their efficiency through the use of technology.

## Self-employment

Some examples of the use of ICT within a self-employed context are:

- Creating invoices to send to customers.
- Designing a logo and letter heading.
- Designing posters and leaflets to advertise your services.
- Developing business websites to advertise products and services.
- Producing a standard letters to give a professional image to a small enterprise.
- Maintaining business accounts.
- Communicating with customers through e-mail received on a PDA.
- Accessing technical product information on the World Wide Web.
- Submitting self-assessment tax returns online.

## Paid employment

Some examples of the use of ICT within an employed context are:

- Planning a journey for your manager using online timetables and maps.
- Keeping an electronic diary, things-to-do lists and the electronic address book to ensure good time management.
- Creating a mail group for a team so that e-mails can be sent to everyone in a group or team.
- Using a project management application to create a visual work plan.
- Securing the business's information through security systems, including being aware of your responsibilities under the Data Protection Act.
- Preparing a presentation for a business meeting.

## Unpaid (voluntary work)

Some examples of the use of ICT within a volunteer context are:

- Keeping records of trustee meetings.
- Maintaining the records of donations made to the organisation.
- Producing a volunteer rota to ensure that reception is covered during the opening hours.

- Creating an organisation website.
- Designing leaflets to advertise services or provide information to clients.
- Digital photographs of organisational activities to illustrate web pages, leaflets and other publications.

There are many different possible tasks involving employment and these will vary according to the nature of the work. It is probably sensible to ask learners to bring examples of tasks they wish to use ICT to complete. This may provide the basis for an individual project. It is useful to consider the potential project against the course curriculum and assessment criteria to ensure that it matches. This will save a lot of effort and ensures the learner's purpose is met and also the course standards are covered.

# Domestic and everyday life

Technology is increasingly a part of people's lives, with ICT now a key ingredient in society. Almost everywhere you go computers can play a role. Many shopping centres provide access to information through computer displays involving users in understanding navigation techniques. You can buy train tickets via automatic systems, book holidays online, place orders for goods by e-mail and many other tasks. They require people who are confident and competent users of a wide range of applications and systems. The list of examples below is not exhaustive but may serve to illustrate possible ways of providing context in this area.

## Examples

1. **Keep family financial records.**
2. **Shop online.**
3. **E-mail family and friends to allow you to send family photographs.**
4. **Send an electronic message to a radio or television programme in order to take part.**
5. **Locate information about the many and varied aspects of everyday life.**
6. **Interests and hobbies (e.g. gardening, collecting, genealogy, cookery, wine making and photography).**
7. **Plan holidays (e.g. booking hotels).**
8. **Locate information about events to attend (e.g. theatre programmes).**
9. **Seek assistance with DIY projects.**
10. **Locate information about health.**
11. **Book appointments with doctors and dentists.**
12. **Help children to prepare their assignments.**

People employ a wide range of technology in their lives. They may simply send text messages while listening to digital music. However, they are likely to use the World Wide Web to complete crosswords, help their children with their homework, download music, shop online, seek weather information, find maps to plan journeys or book theatre tickets. Technology in the home is growing rapidly and people are using it as a normal part of their lives. The use of ICT by children means that parents need the skills to protect their children from the offensive content within the World Wide Web. This is also related to understanding how to ensure systems are free from virus attack and spyware.

# Leisure

ICT can assist a very wide range of interests, activities and hobbies. You can, for example, get the cricket scores by visiting the BBC website, read the text commentary of a football match, listen to Internet radio, e-mail your answer to a general knowledge quiz, discuss the latest research findings in astronomy, construct a database to keep records of your collection or design posters to advertise your groups meetings.

Teachers are now starting to employ video cameras in their work. When you are learning to dance you can receive visual feedback on how to position your feet. A graphic tablet can help you design a piece of pottery while a digital camera allows you to record a journey in detail. The World Wide Web offers the opportunity for artists and writers to publish their work online. There has been a considerable growth in online publishers who will sell your writing and of course you could set up your own website. This suggests that people need to understand how to convert word processor files into Acrobat or other formats suitable for electronic publishing.

The list of examples below serves to illustrate possible ways of providing context in this area.

## Examples

1. *Many hobbies (e.g. bird watching, collecting stamps and aircraft spotting) require you to keep records. Designing a database is very useful since it allows you to sort records and present them in the desired form (e.g. birds seen in the last month). A database can be searched, queried and used as a source for reports.*
2. *Sending e-mails to members of a group or society to inform them of meetings, special developments and opportunities.*
3. *The World Wide Web can provide sources of inspiration for arts and crafts to assist you to create works of art (e.g. painting, poetry and prose).*
4. *Digital photography can relate to many different hobbies and interests (e.g. walking, historic buildings, sport and astronomy). To gain the maximum benefit, people need to have the skills to edit images and store them.*
5. *There are many sources of online information to plan trips of all types. You may simply want to travel by train, book a hotel or view a map, but you could also plan an international holiday to walk a battlefield or see whales.*

There are many hobbies and leisure interests that people follow and similarly there is a variety of technology available to assist these activities.

# Education and training

ICT is increasingly being employed to support and deliver learning in all parts of education and training. Children are assisted through technology to learn, while online learning supports workers to be trained at their workplaces. Universities are already using e-learning methods to help students study, while many people use the World Wide Web for informal learning. People are often motivated to learn about ICT so that they can assist their children's education as well as their own. Many companies provide training using online and other forms of e-learning which allows them to meet the immediate needs of employees (i.e. just in time training). There is clearly a trend towards the integration of technology with education and training so the future is likely to see more links.

The list of examples below is not exhaustive, but shows some potential ways of providing context in this area.

## Examples

1. *Parents can use government websites (e.g. Department for Education and Skills) to find information about developments effecting the education of their children.*
2. *There are many computer-based learning products available to support adults self-study in numerous subjects and particularly ICT.*
3. *An important part of many education and training programmes is online communication since this allows groups of learners to support each other.*
4. *There are a variety of revision aids provided online aimed at helping children to study for examinations, although more adult resources are becoming available. These take various forms (e.g. science simulations and tutorials), and cover both informal and formal learning.*
5. *There is now access to many leading libraries and museums online to provide you with a wide range of learning resources.*

While there is considerable potential for ICT to assist learning, this does assume that learners have both ICT and suitable learning skills (Clarke, 2004). ICT can help people to study by helping them to present their work effectively, access resources, communicate with their peers and organise their learning (Clarke, 2005).

In order to benefit from the possibilities that technology offers, learners need to be competent and confident users of ICT. They need to be able to locate resources online (i.e. have extensive search skills), communicate (i.e. use e-mail including managing their messages), use a range of applications (e.g. word processing) and manage their systems (e.g. create effective folder and file structures).

## Developing materials

An important way of incorporating context into ICT programmes is to develop learning materials and resources focused on the learner's purpose and interests. These can take a variety of forms including:

- work sheets;
- web searchers;
- Webquests;
- case studies;
- discussion topics;
- group activities;
- peer activities;
- individual assignments.

## Work sheets

Work sheets are used extensively in ICT courses to help learners explore and practise using applications. They are very versatile in that they can be simple (e.g. enter a few sentences into a word processor) or complex (e.g. design a web page). They can offer step-by-step guides to the task or offer the learning objectives with a few tips on how to proceed, so can prove a flexible resource. Their main limitations are that they tend to be mechanical in helping people to learn narrow specific skills without gaining an appreciation of the wider issues. However, they can address precise contexts. Most worksheets are intended for individual use.

## Web searchers

These are essentially challenges to learners (i.e. individuals or groups) to find information. They are aimed at the development of search techniques, but due to the enormous range of subjects on the World Wide Web can fit almost any context. The information discovered can be used as a resource for other activities such as writing with a word processor, analysing numerical information with a spreadsheet or designing a publication.

## Webquests

Webquests allow you to exploit the vast resources available on the World Wide Web. They are focused on analysing the available information rather than locating it so are a good approach when assisting learners judge the quality of website contents. However, the focus of the Webquest may align with almost any context (e.g. health, politics, sport, children and work). The outcomes of the quest can be used as a source for other actions.

## Case studies

A case study allows a focus on a specific experience and activity (e.g. designing a poster to advertise a village fete). They are therefore useful devices to provide context and purpose. They enable learners to gain experience of new situations. Learners seeking to change occupations can build their understanding of the new situation through the case study (e.g. produce a set of minutes from a digital transcript following a standard template, plan a business trip for a senior manager and organise a meeting through e-mail). Case studies can be narrow or wide, so provide flexibility in delivery.

## Discussion topics

ICT courses have been criticised for concentrating on individual activities and ignoring the potential of group work. A discussion topic can be employed by the whole class or small groups to consider a specific issue. They therefore have the potential to consider a particular context or purpose. Some examples are:

- how do you ensure the security of your information?
- what do you do to protect your health and safety when using ICT?
- what application would you use to produce a ten page booklet and why?

The limitation of discussion is that ICT is essentially a practical subject involving the operation of equipment. A discussion will help to develop knowledge but not skill.

## Group and peer activities

Group activities are not widely used in ICT programmes, partially due to the individual nature of the computer workstations. There are, nevertheless, ways to overcome this limitation such as:

- using a video projector so that a whole group can see what is happening;
- limiting the group size to two or three so that everyone can see the display;
- using networks so that each group member can simultaneously access the same application and resources;
- using voting systems which are are now available to allow groups to interact through technology.

A major benefit of group work is that learners have the help of several colleagues rather than being restricted to their own resources. The different experiences of the topic across the group can be applied to solve the problem with everyone learning from each other.

## Individual assignments

Individual exercises are by far the most frequently used approaches in ICT courses. This is probably driven by the nature of computer systems that are designed for single use. Learners need to acquire personal confidence, skills and knowledge so a large element of individualised work is probably appropriate. Exercises and activities can be focused on specific contexts and purposes. Perhaps the most effective is to develop an activity based on a challenge the learners are actually facing, so they should be asked to offer tasks they want to achieve (e.g. write a letter applying for a job, buy an online product or edit a digital photograph)

## Context:

# a summary of key points

____ *Adults have many reasons for wishing to learn about ICT. These reasons are related to a range of factors, but one way of considering learners' context is through the Skills for Life standards.*

____ *An important way of incorporating individual learners' context in ICT programmes is to ask them to identify tasks they would like to carry out. These can then form the basis of learning activities.*

____ *Learning materials can take a number of forms from an individual worksheet to an online quest. They can all be designed to provide learning with a focus on a particular context or purpose.*

# 6 INTEGRATING ICT IN OTHER SUBJECTS

## Introduction

Chapter 3 introduced the possibilities of integrating or embedding ICT in another subject, that is, learning ICT skills through subjects such as local history, literacy or numeracy, financial education or creative writing. Many learners are interested in learning through the medium of ICT. Adults trying to improve their reading and writing are often motivated to learn through technology, essentially by using e-learning which is rapidly spreading across all parts of education and training. ICT is therefore being integrated across the whole curriculum so the opportunity to embed technology is available within a wide range of subjects.

The process of learning through technology can lead to improving and extending the learners' ICT skills. However, to meet specific ICT objectives requires both subjects to be carefully mapped against standards so the learners' progress can be identified. It is the equivalent of undertaking a joint honours degree compared to a single subject degree with the added complexity that the subjects are integrated. An important point to realise is that standards for different subjects are normally developed without any consideration of how they relate to each other. This means that there is no reason to expect that items at Entry Level 3 in one subject will directly relate to the same level in another one. It is often the case that there is no match. Equally, the learners' needs across the two subjects may not relate. It is perfectly possible for an individual to be studying at Entry Level 3 in numeracy while their ICT needs are at Level 2. This obviously poses practical challenges which need to be overcome in order to embed the subjects.

Learning ICT with another subject has the following advantages.

- **Motivational** – ICT may motivate learners. Those students seeking to learn the use of technology to achieve a goal will link their studies to another subject that interests them and thus also provide motivation.
- **Contextual** – ICT user skills are always applied so it is appropriate to learn ICT in a context suitable for the learner.
- **Natural** – ICT skills and knowledge are employed in specific situations (e.g. work).
- **Purposeful** – ICT learning is strongly linked to purposes relevant to the learner.
- **Supportive** – ICT can help support and deliver learning.
- **Economical** – studying two useful subjects is often more effective than learning about them individually.

# Adult literacy

The Adult Literacy Core Curriculum document contains a wide range of references to the application of ICT in support of developing literacy skills and knowledge. These are often contained in suggestions for learning activities. They cover the whole curriculum from Entry Levels to Level 2, covering speaking and listening, reading and writing. They include:

- word processing;
- text messaging;
- using CD-ROMs;
- presentation applications;
- e-mail messages;
- digital sound recording;
- online radio broadcasts;
- searching the World Wide Web;
- considering the content of web pages;
- spell checking;
- digital video;
- voice mail messages.

This simple list suggests that there is considerable potential to develop ICT skills and knowledge through the application of technology to assist learners develop their literacy skills. It includes a range of applications and hardware, and breaks away from the stereotypical approach of word processing, spreadsheets and databases into a richer and more interesting mix. Let's consider some example activities using ICT within adult literacy, how they link to ICT and relate to the ICT Skill for Life standard.

## Word processing

There is considerable potential for using word processing as an aid to learning in adult literacy. In the Core Curriculum document many sample activities relate to the use of word processing. The Write to Communicate aspects of the standard lend themselves to the application of word processing in a number of different ways. However, there is probably a need for the learners to have some basic word processing skills before starting to embed the two subjects together.

## *Examples*

*At adult literacy Entry Level, examples of electronic text can be provided so that learners can focus on activities such as punctuation, without the need to enter large amounts of text. At higher levels, learners can be asked to write letters, design advertising flyers and compose stories. These all involve practising entering and editing text. This aligns with ICT Skill for Life standard at a variety of levels depending on the complexity of the task such as:*

1. *Entry Level 2, Developing and presenting information, 6.1, 6.2 and 7.1 – these are all associated with entering and presenting written work.*

2. *Level 1, Developing and presenting information, 6a.1, 6a.2, 6a.3 and 6a.4 – these are all linked to developing a document and include editing and formatting it.*

There are several other potential links such as:

- case sensitivity;
- tables;
- tracking changes to show alterations which help a teacher to review work;
- lists;
- inserting images;
- line spacing;
- paragraphs;
- borders;
- find and replace.

## Text messaging

Text messaging is now a familiar part of people's lives. It involves both reading and writing simple sentences, and initially it is probably useful at Entry Level I for writing short messages and at Entry Level 2 for reading replies or new messages sent to the learner. These activities align with the ICT Skill for Life standard at Entry Level 2.

Many learners will already have text messaging skills, so there is the possibility of enhancing these straightforward tasks so that a rich communication can take place within the group of learners. It is also possible to extend the programme sessions by learners continuing to discuss ideas through text messaging between face-to-face meetings. There is also the added bonus that you can keep them informed about changes to the course and remind them of assessment dates or other matters.

Learners who become confident and competent users of text messages are developing skills and understanding that can be transferred to other situations (e.g. understanding icons and interfaces) and in the process assist with the development of learning skills.

## Voice mail messages

The use of voice mail is a natural extension of text messaging. Mobile phones have the facility to leave voice messages when the phone is engaged or switched off, which allows learners to practise leaving and listening to messages. They can send each other messages and analyse the clarity, use of language and other factors.

Learners who become confident and competent senders and receivers of voice messages are developing skills and understanding that can be transferred to other situations (e.g. understanding icons, controls and interfaces). These align with the ICT Skill for Life standards in the Using of ICT Systems at entry levels.

# Using CD-ROMs

Adults improving their literacy skills have wide ranging interests. It is important to maintain their motivation by offering them opportunities to improve their reading and writing through material relevant to their needs. CD-ROMs are available with resources covering many different subjects and interests (e.g. clip art collections, newspaper archives, history and finance). In terms of ICT skills the learners have opportunities to find information through searching the resources, which is part of the ICT Skill for Life standard at all levels. In addition the application of the resources can link to other aspects of the standard such as developing and presenting information:

- copying and pasting;
- laying out information;
- editing.

There are many opportunities to make links since the CD-ROMs are essentially a resource which you can employ in many different ways.

# Presentation applications

A key element in both literacy and ICT standards is the presentation of information in order to communicate. The use of presentation applications is therefore appropriate to both subjects. Presentation applications are often multimedia so speech can be incorporated, providing opportunities for learners to practise their spoken communication.

The design of a presentation involves many actions that link to ICT and literacy such as:

- use of upper and lower case;
- use of bold, italics and underlining to emphasise words and phrases;
- fonts and character sizes;
- alignment of text;
- using pictures with text.

Presentations can be developed about any subjects that meet individual and group interests. Presentation applications can be used by individuals, pairs of learners, small groups or even as part of whole class exercises. They are flexible and can be made into engaging and fun activities.

## E-mail messages

E-mail has become a significant communication channel, making it an important element in adult literacy. It is also a potentially powerful way of assisting learning to develop reading and writing skills. E-mail allows a dialogue to be undertaken within and outside of the group. In a way, it can simulate the exchange of correspondence with the advantage that timescales are compressed (i.e. you don't have to wait for the letter to be transported). E-mail provides learners with the means to practise their writing skills and also consider the importance of punctuation and layout.

From the ICT perspective, e-mail is a key element in exchanging information aspects of the ICT Skill for Life standard and a wide range of ICT qualifications. By linking it to a purposeful context it will motivate learners and help them realise the importance of not simply sending and receiving messages but also understanding the need to manage them through organising files and folders and keeping address books. This allows a link into file management which is often an area that learners find difficult to understand. These types of activities link to the ICT Skill for Life standard in Using ICT Systems and probably at Entry Level 3 to Level 2, depending on the nature of the activities.

## Digital sound recording

Digital sound recording devices are now available in many forms making it possible to provide a whole class with hand-held devices that can be carried anywhere. They allow individuals to record their own speech, conversations and sounds. They are ideal for learners undertaking a project or assignment during the session or between sessions. Learners could be asked to undertake a project that involves interviewing other people (e.g. their peers, family and friends) or investigating an issue that involves them in recording their own comments (e.g. congestion in a town centre). There are many opportunities to practise communication, and listening to your own questions or comments is a useful way to gain feedback about your spoken communications.

The degree of complexity can be varied to meet the needs of the learners. It can simply be two learners reading out messages to each other so that they can discuss each other's delivery, a learner undertaking an interview or the recording of a conversation. Recording allows for a detailed review to be undertaken.

In terms of ICT, digital sound recording can be motivating, not least in the context of the large number of people who listen to digital music. It provides many opportunities to develop skills such as:

- using controls;
- recognising icons and new interfaces (i.e. transferring learning to a new situation);
- saving sound files on a computer and making the link to why backing up data is important;
- management of files.

## Online radio broadcasts

The Internet offers access to a wide range of different sources of broadcasting so adult literacy learners can listen to subjects that interest them (e.g. sport, soap operas, drama and news). This gives them the possibility of assessing the effectiveness of the delivery in a range of contexts. This could be an individual, paired or small group exercise. Locating and using online radio is also rich in ICT possibilities in that it is purposeful, with the individuals seeking a broadcast that meets their needs and requires them to practise a variety of useful skills and apply their understanding of the Internet. It will require learners to:

- search the World Wide Web;
- navigate websites and interact with them;
- consider the content of web pages;
- use equipment (e.g. headphones).

These types of activities link to the ICT Skill for Life standard in Using ICT Systems, probably at Entry Level 3 to Level 2, as well as finding information aspects at Level 1, depending on the nature of the activities.

## Spell checking

Almost all applications offer some form of spell checker and, in some cases, thesaurus and grammar checkers. In many ICT qualifications there is a requirement that users are able to use these features and understand their limitations. In adult literacy, spelling and grammar checkers are also important in that learners need to be able to understand their use. They identify possible errors and the user needs to make a decision about the options suggested.

## Digital images and video

Digital cameras are widely available and often incorporate sound recording and video. Many learners will have had some experience with them. They have the potential to engage and motivate people studying literacy and ICT. A class can be provided with cameras for use in the classroom and between sessions. They have broadly similar possibilities to the use of digital sound recorders, but with the additional benefit of capturing still and moving images. They can help learners carry out assignments in or between sessions. Learners could be asked to undertake a project to investigate a topic and present a report of their findings (e.g. public transport).

The degree of complexity can be varied to meet the needs of the learners. It can simply be a task to gather images of a topic to be used to illustrate a composition, or an investigation to develop a report including a presentation.

In terms of ICT, digital photography can be motivating and provides many opportunities to develop skills such as:

- using controls;
- recognising icons and new interfaces (i.e. transferring learning to a new situation);

- editing images;
- producing resources for presentations, desktop publishing and Web page design;
- saving image files on a computer and making the link to why backing up data is important;
- management of files.

These types of activities link to the ICT Skill for Life standard in Using ICT Systems and Developing and Presenting Information across Entry Level 3 to Level 2, depending on the nature of the activities.

# Adult numeracy

The Adult Numeracy Core Curriculum document contains references to the application of ICT in support of developing numeracy skills and knowledge and are often contained in suggestions for learning activities. They span the whole curriculum from Entry Levels to Level 2, covering whole numbers, fractions, decimals and percentages, common measures, shape and space, data and statistical measures and probability. They include:

- spreadsheets;
- calculators;
- digital clocks;
- graphs and charts;
- word processors;
- websites;
- painting and drawing.

## Spreadsheets

There is a fairly obvious link between numeracy and spreadsheets. The link exists across all the levels in that at entry levels the learners can be provided with complete numerical models to interact with, while at higher levels they can be asked to develop the model. There are many possible applications of spreadsheets that will assist learners develop their numeracy while also adding to their ICT skills and understanding.

At entry level a model of family expenditure could be provided into which the learners need to enter their own costs. This would allow them to explore the relationships between certain types of expenditure and their overall budget. In terms of ICT skills they would gain an understanding of entering information, correcting mistakes, the structure of the sheet (i.e. cells, rows and columns) and probably printing. This aligns with ICT Skill for Life at Entry Level 3.

There are also more advanced uses of spreadsheets with learners developing their own model of family expenditure, which involves them in using mathematical operators such as addition and division. It could also involve them in developing an understanding of averages and constructing formulas. Their ICT skills could also cover:

- entering numerical data;
- developing formulas;
- using functions (e.g. SUM);
- sorting;
- adjusting decimal places;
- currency;
- replication;
- printing;
- layout (e.g. adjusting the size of rows and columns);
- fonts and character sizes.

There is considerable potential in integrating numeracy with spreadsheets. In addition PDAs often have spreadsheet applications so that the embedding could be accomplished using portable equipment rather than desktops and laptops. This would widen possibilities for helping learners to practise transferring skills between systems.

## Calculators

Calculators have been playing a part in mathematics for many years. There are clearly possibilities of helping learners gain an understanding of interfaces, icons and memory through the use of a calculator. In addition, operating systems such as Microsoft Windows provide an on-screen calculator so that it should be possible to practise in two different but related environments. In terms of ICT Skill for Life this would mainly be linked to Entry Level 1 and 2, Using ICT Systems and Developing and Presenting Information.

## Digital clocks

Electronic clocks offer similar possibilities to calculators in that using them to help learners appreciate digital time and a 24 hour clock also allows them to practise interacting with an interface (e.g. recognising icons and controls). There are probably several other devices of this type that could contribute to developing numeracy and ICT skills.

## Graphs and charts

The Adult Numeracy Core Curriculum also includes shape and space. Charts and graphs applications enable learners to construct 2- and 3-D images that relate to specific numerical data. This allows both numeracy and ICT skills to be integrated. Producing 3-D images requires the learners to be able to:

- select data (e.g. highlight areas of a spreadsheet);
- choose a chart or graph type (e.g. pie chart);

- employ titles, legends and data labels;
- understand axes;
- edit charts and graphs.

These are largely Level I and 2 skills and knowledge. Figure I5 illustrates a 3-D chart.

## Hours worked

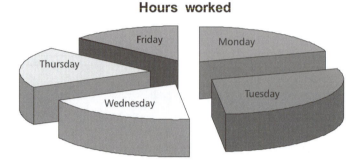

Fig. I5 3-D chart

# Word processors

Word processors can also play a part in adult numeracy through their ability to construct tables and list items in order. A table can be used to produce:

- a set of conversions (e.g. inches into centimetres);
- equivalent values (e.g. decimals, fractions and percentages) – Figure I6 illustrates a table;
- comparisons of values (e.g. interest rates).

These can be used at different levels. At entry level they can be provided for learners to use while at more advanced levels they can be asked to construct them.

| Decimals | Fractions | Percentages |
|----------|-----------|-------------|
| 0.125 | 1/8 | 12.5% |
| 0.25 | 1/4 | 25% |
| 0.375 | 3/8 | 37.5% |
| 0.5 | ½ | 50% |
| 0.625 | 5/8 | 62.5% |
| 0.75 | ¾ | 75% |
| 0.875 | 7/8 | 87.5% |
| 1 | 1 | 100% |

Fig. I6 Equivalence table

These types of activities allow you to develop some of the following ICT skills:

- insert table;
- enter data into a table;
- format a table;
- insert rows and columns;

- use autofit options;
- print table.

In addition to constructing tables it is possible to use word processing to produce ordered lists of items or use numbers to label a list. Learners can increase their understanding of size and value while developing ICT skills in respect of using bullets and numbering functions.

## Websites

The main role of websites in adult numeracy is to provide learners with relevant information such as:

- local council expenditure;
- currency exchange rates;
- price of goods (i.e. shopping website);
- tax and national insurance rates.

This allows them to learn numeracy skills with up-to-date and relevant information. In terms of ICT skills there is the potential to practise:

- searching for information using simple and complex search methods with a variety of search engines;
- searching websites using local search engines;
- navigating websites (i.e. forward, back and hyperlinks);
- printing web pages;
- using favorites to save addresses of useful web pages.

These are at Level I Finding and Exchanging Information ICT Skill for Life standards.

## Painting and drawing

To appreciate shape and space it is often useful for the learner to be able to draw the shape and manipulate the space. Painting and drawing applications and functions offer the means to construct a wide variety of shapes. Microsoft Word offers functions to draw rectangles, ovals and many standard objects, while Windows Paint provides a straightforward tool to produce shapes of your choosing. There are also many other powerful tools.

## ESOL

The application of different forms of computer-based learning to develop second language skills has a long history covering a large part of the last two decades, so this may well be an indication that this pairing will be successful. The Adult ESOL Core Curriculum document contains a wide range of references to the application of ICT in support of developing language skills and knowledge. These are often contained in suggestions for learning activities. They cover the whole curriculum from Entry

Levels to Level 2 covering speaking and listening, reading and writing. In addition there is the experience gained in using technology in language learning. Some applications of ICT that would integrate with ESOL are:

- digital video and still photography;
- digital sound;
- databases;
- word processing;
- World Wide Web.

There is obviously a strong relationship between the use of ICT within literacy and ESOL. The examples given in the earlier section on literacy will transfer to a large extent to ESOL. In addition the motivation to learn to use ICT is likely to be important with adults seeking to learn English in that the skills of using technology are basic to gaining employment, which for many learners will be a key reason for coming to the United Kingdom.

## Digital video and still photography

An important part of learning any language lies in developing the basic skills of living in the society in which the language is being used. This involves understanding and being able to communicate about everyday events such as using public transport, understanding timetables, reading signs, shopping, taking children to school and communicating with public agencies. A powerful way of learning the relevant language and associated knowledge is to carry out projects or assignments in small groups. A video camera can provide a central point for these tasks, such as investigating how public transport is organised. It allows learners to capture information, study it later and share it with others.

In terms of ICT the use of a camera offers opportunities to learn about:

- using controls;
- recognising icons and new interfaces (e.g. transferring learning to a new situation);
- editing images;
- producing resources for presentations, desktop publishing and web page design;
- saving image files on a computer and making the link to why backing up data is important;
- management of files.

These types of activities link to the ICT Skill for Life standard in Using ICT Systems and Developing and Presenting Information across Entry Level 3 to Level 2, depending on the nature of the activities.

In addition learners can watch video films to help them understand speech and visual language (e.g. gestures). This again offers the possibility of transferring understanding of icons, interfaces and controls to new situations. To gain confidence and skills in transferring learning requires as many opportunities to practise as can be provided. Still images provide a stimulus for learners to write short stories, as an aid to conversation and give context for language.

## Digital sound

Digital sound recorders are available in hand-held sizes, so learners can both listen to English and practise their speech with the facility to listen to their own words and compare with a first language speaker previously recorded.

In terms of ICT, digital sound recording provides many chances to develop skills such as:

- using controls;
- recognising icons and new interfaces;
- saving sound files on a computer and making the link to why backing up data is important;
- management of files.

## Databases and spreadsheets

Entering English into applications allows learners to practise correct spelling, punctuation and grammar. It is important with adults to provide appropriate stimuli that are relevant and interesting to them. Entering data into a database or spreadsheet about a survey or investigation that they have undertaken may serve these purposes. It also provides practice in using different applications and helps learners identify the similarities and differences between them.

## Word processing

There is considerable potential to use word processing in ESOL. In many ways this is similar to adult literacy in that it is a tool for developing and presenting writing and this is key to both subjects. There are additional features of some word processors (e.g. Microsoft Word) to translate English into some other languages and these may be helpful.

## E-mail

Language is about communication so e-mail offers learners the chance to practise their written English as part of a conversation. It is likely to motivate learners in that it will also allow them to communicate easily with their families and friends in their countries of origin. Email is useful to ESOL users in broadly the same way as for adult literacy students.

## Online radio

The opportunity to listen to spoken English is very useful when learning to understand the language. Access to online radio broadcasts offers a wide selection of subjects to listen to that maximise relevance and interests to learners. It will require learners to be able to search the World Wide Web, navigate websites and use equipment (e.g. headphones). These types of activities link to the ICT Skill for Life standard in Using ICT Systems, probably at Entry Level 3 to Level 2, as well as finding information aspects at Level I, depending on the nature of the activities.

## World Wide Web

There is always the need for more resources to stimulate learners and provide them with a source to write about, study or speak in relation to. The potential of the World Wide Web to offer an enormous library of material is a major aid in ESOL. There is also the additional benefit of sites written in the learner's first language so they have the additional motivation of news from home. There are sites which offer translation into English and a practical aid to living in the United Kingdom by providing useful information. This gives many possibilities for improving searching skills, navigating websites, printing pages, downloading files and saving information. These activities relate to the ICT Skills for Life standard in respect of Using ICT systems and Finding and Exchanging Information from Entry Level 3 to Level 2, depending on the complexity of the tasks.

## Dictionaries and computer-based learning

There is a variety of aids to learning English such as portable electronic dictionaries and computer-based learning materials. These offer the possibilities of operating a range of ICT systems, thus assisting the transfer of skills and understanding to new situations.

# Other subjects

There are various other subjects in which ICT could be embedded or integrated so that both ICT and the subject skills and knowledge can be achieved. Some possibilities are:

- Financial Education – there is a relationship between adult numeracy and financial education (Clarke, 2006).
- Local history – the World Wide Web will provide an important source of information while databases offer the functionality to record findings, with desktop publishing the means to disseminate outcomes to a wider audience.
- Creative writing – the word processor is probably central to this subject, but publishing online provides a link to web page and site design.

## *Integrating ICT in other subjects:*

# a summary of key points

—— *There are several advantages of learning ICT within another subject.*

—— *Studying two useful subjects together is often more effective than learning about them individually.*

—— *Preparation is essential for embedding ICT in other subjects. It is vital to map standards carefully against each other.*

—— *It is important to consider the learners' needs in relation to both subjects and identify activities that integrate them together.*

—— *There are many opportunities to link ICT with adult literacy, numeracy, ESOL and other subjects.*

—— *Many different technologies can be integrated, such as word processing, digital photography, spreadsheets, websites and e-mail.*

# 7 SUPPORT

## Introduction

Learners who are new to ICT will often need to be supported in order to succeed. ICT is a practical subject where learners will often need to work on individual projects which require them to spend time looking at a computer display, with little opportunity to interact with other learners. This is not the best learning practice since being aware of what peers are doing, listening to the questions they ask and being able to ask each other for help are all supportive elements in learning. It is vital that tutors work actively to counter the negative aspects of working individually on a computer.

New ICT learners may lack confidence in their ability to learn about ICT. Many adults still have little experience of technology and a large proportion give this as a reason for their lack of confidence. It is therefore important to ensure that they are well supported so that self-esteem and confidence grow with their learning. This is important in all contexts, but approaches such as drop-in centres especially need to have excellent support in place to ensure good retention rates. When learners encounter a problem they will often need help to resolve it. This should be provided in a form that encourages them to develop problem solving skills. Many learners complain that more experienced users and tutors help them, but in a way that does not allow them to understand the problem so they can deal with it themselves. This is sometimes linked to the speed at which the correction is undertaken, the jargon employed or simply that they could not see what happened owing to the limited visibility surrounding the computer system.

All users will encounter new situations so it is important that they are confident enough to explore and identify their own solutions. This will build self-assurance and independence which are key components in a capable ICT user. While provision of support has the potential to assist the growth of confidence, it can unfortunately also hinder the process if the user becomes dependent. Learners need to realise that problems and difficulties are a natural part of ICT, to be overcome as they are encountered. Here are some of the main characteristics of support.

- **Timely** – few things are more de-motivating than having to wait for help when you have reached a stage where you cannot progress. It is vital that support can be quickly provided.

- **Pro-active** – many learners will not want to show that they have a problem, so it is important to be able to diagnose when help is needed and offer it, ideally before they have to request assistance.

- **Multiple source** – the tutor or other support workers are obviously a major source of assistance but other learners, software and learning materials can also be used. It has been widely accepted that receptionists in a learning centre can often provide appropriate support in the many small issues that learners may find puzzling. Application software help systems are a useful source of support if the learners understand how to use them.

- **Flexible** – support needs to be adaptable to meet different situations. This may mean that you develop a handout with common problems or perhaps as part of the course. Record each problem encountered so that the whole group benefits from identifying new issues. This will help learners who are reluctant to ask for help to see that it is natural and helpful to the whole group.

- **Personalised** – learners are individuals and need to be treated in a way that meets their individual needs. Support needs to be offered in a way that is appropriate to the individual.

All learners will need some support from time to time. Many learners will identify the tutor as the most useful aid to their learning. It is therefore important to be available and to treat problems as an opportunity to help the learners to understand ICT. It is often useful to make a question from an individual an example for the whole group to learn from. This needs to be done with care to avoid belittling the individual, but if you make it clear that this is an opportunity to show everyone an important point, this should be avoided. I normally ask the person's permission to reveal the problem (e.g. this is a key point that everyone will encounter. Do you mind if I use you as an example to help everyone?).

## Key issues

Some key issues to consider in learning support are:

- assistance;
- problem solving;
- observation;
- learning points;
- between sessions;
- peer support;
- mentoring and coaching;
- students with disabilities (e.g. assistive technology);
- left-handed learners;
- individual support;
- tutor support (e.g. e-learning content);
- role of volunteers;
- information, advice and guidance for learners;
- personalisation.

## Assistance

When giving assistance it is important to allow the learner to carry out the required actions. This will help them remember how to deal with the problem on another occasion. It is important to avoid taking over their computer and doing it for them. Try to:

- get them to solve the problem by asking questions so they work out the solution for themselves;
- relate the problem to other things they have encountered so that they understand relationships and are encouraged to transfer their understanding to new situations;
- systematically explain the solution and give them step-by-step instruction to carry out the actions (this will help them to remember what to do);
- be positive about the fact that everyone encounters problems and that the key is not to be discouraged.

## Problem solving

An important part of becoming an independent, capable ICT user is the ability to solve problems which you encounter (e.g. how does this new version of the application allow me to … ?). The process of learners asking for help provides you with a range of opportunities to develop their problem-solving skills. The nature of each problem that the learners find difficult helps you to assess their existing skills and needs. Each example gives you the opportunity to explain how to deal with it through a systematic approach. This process allows you to integrate a problem-solving approach in the programme. However, you may wish to supplement it with direct input or handouts giving a suggested approach to handling troubles.

As you gain experience you will develop a detailed understanding of the nature of problems that new ICT users face or find difficult. This experience is useful in helping you to support them since you can forewarn them, offer ways to overcome the problem or modify your teaching so they never encounter them. Appendix I (page 115) gives a short list of possible problems which new ICT users may encounter.

A small but useful activity at the start of a programme is to make it clear that it is natural to ask for help from time to time and to react to requests as if they were perfectly normal. It is useful to ask the group if they have any questions, and welcome the ones asked so that you encourage the whole process.

## Observation

Many learners are reluctant to ask for help so it is important to observe your group constantly in order to identify those learners who are struggling or puzzled. This is not easy since they will almost certainly be facing a computer and you may well be able to see only their backs or the computer. It is therefore useful to move around the room in order to give yourself different views of the learners. It is also less of a challenge to ask a tutor for assistance when they are only a few feet away than to summon you from across the room, thus informing the whole group that they have a problem.

It is often effective to combine observation with systematically asking each learner about his or her progress. This provides them with an opportunity to ask questions about their concerns as well as providing you with a means of monitoring progress.

## Learning points

Every question you are asked and each problem a learner encounters can be used as a learning point to reinforce some aspect of ICT. You may want to:

- use the example to explain to the whole group – this is potentially very powerful, but avoid breaking the concentration of the group too often;
- record all the difficulties on a visual aid (e.g. electronic whiteboard) so that you develop a running record for everyone to learn from (this may form the basis of a handout for the next group of learners or the basis of a review session).

Basically, be positive and treat each problem encountered as an opportunity to help the learning programme.

## Between sessions

Many learners will want to practise between the formal sessions, so consider how you can help them make the most of the opportunity. It is useful to:

- explain where they can gain access to ICT equipment between sessions;
- provide exercises to take away;
- suggest self-help books or other materials;
- explain how the college learning centre works.

Their circumstances and the facilities that you have will place limitations on what you can offer, but don't ignore the possibility. However, many adult learners will have busy lives and will be unable to practise.

## Peer support

Most learners, at least initially, will be reluctant to ask you questions but are likely to ask questions of their peers since this is far less threatening. People will naturally help each other so peer support should be relatively straightforward to achieve. However, you can do a lot to hinder it by not thinking through your initial process of starting the course. It is important to encourage learners to get to know each other and remember each others' names. The introductory session is an excellent opportunity to get peer support underway. You might:

- ask everyone to introduce themselves;
- divide the group into pairs and ask them to prepare to introduce their partner;

- provide learners with name cards or badges – barriers are reduced if you know a person's name;
- ask each person to take a digital photograph of another member of the group and produce a class name sheet with a photograph alongside the names (this is fun and will break the ice effectively);
- ask each person to explain what they want to achieve from the course and get them to compare their motives;
- provide a taster session giving the group the opportunity to try lots of different technology (e.g. digital cameras, printers, scanners, Internet etc.) so that they have the opportunity to meet everyone.

These actions can obviously be combined and they serve more than one purpose. A taster session can help you assess each learner's existing skills and confidence. All of them offer a way to break down barriers and encourage people to communicate.

Other actions you can take to develop peer support include:

- consider the layout of the room and try to position learners so it is easy to talk to each other and encourage them to do so;
- employ group and paired exercises to encourage mutual support;
- provide breaks so there is an opportunity to meet people who are sitting in other parts of the room.

You can probably think of other actions that will bring people together and offer opportunities to communicate.

## Mentoring and coaching

Mentors and coaches are often employed in large organisations to help develop other members of staff. However, similar roles exist in community and voluntary organisations and within educational institutions. Their role is to advise and guide people, through helping them develop their self-esteem. This is achieved through simply providing a person to discuss matters with, offering a wider perspective, providing access to experience and generally supporting the individuals.

Many new ICT learners have doubts about their abilities to learn to use modern technology, so a mentor who can help them develop their confidence is an important resource. Many companies provide mentors whom learners can contact to discuss their progress. Learning Centres often employ support workers whose role is to mentor and coach individuals while community organisations recruit coaches from successful learners. This latter group has the advantage of having had the same experience as the learners they are mentoring.

## Students with disabilities

Modern operating systems allow you to change the configuration of the system to make it more suitable for individual needs. Microsoft Windows lets you adjust:

- mouse operation;

- keyboard;
- sound effects;
- display.

For disabled learners this may well be essential to assist their learning. It is useful at an early stage in the course to sit down with an individual and show them how to configure the system to meet their needs.

There is also a large range of assistive technologies which may be useful depending on the nature of the disability. These probably require some degree of expertise to decide on but remember that the individuals are expert in their own needs so discuss it with them. There are sources of help in choosing and using assistive technologies in many education and training institutions.

Several national bodies can offer help. In higher, further and special education, Techdis (*www.techdis.ac.uk/*) can offer assistance. In addition organisations such as AbilityNet (*www.abilitynet.org.uk/*) can prove useful.

## Left-handed learners

About ten per cent of the population are left-handed, so in any group you are likely to have at least one person. Operating systems (e.g. Microsoft Windows) allow you to configure the system to suit left-handed people. At an early stage in the course you will want to make the changes so that the learner is not disadvantaged. It also offers a useful way of showing the learner how to configure the system to meet individual preferences.

## Individual support

It is logistically very difficult to provide a single learner in a group with continuous individual support. However, it is possible to offer regular individual help. This is not necessarily from you but by using a variety of resources:

- tutor review of progress;
- learning materials that identify problems and issues and offer help to overcome them;
- support staff and mentors;
- volunteers;
- peer support.

With good organisation and planning, a great deal of individual support can be provided.

## Tutor support

The most valuable supporter of learning is likely to be yourself, the course tutor. Many learners responding to the question 'What is the best support for you?' will answer 'The tutor'. They expect to have your help. The challenge for you is that you have many learners, a syllabus to convey, assessments to undertake and a course to administer. Your time is limited and you need to plan your support so that the benefits are maximised. How can you provide the best support?

The key is to consider the whole course and the many ways that support can be offered. The tutor needs to make the most of the opportunities to provide support through:

- peer support;
- the use of volunteers;
- the design of activities;
- the provision of handouts and other materials.

In many ways the key lies in systematic and detailed preparation. This allows you to concentrate on helping in the most useful ways. It involves two aspects:

- identifying learners who need immediate help to overcome a problem;
- systematically reviewing the progress of all the learners.

It is not always easy to identify when an individual is having problems. They will often not ask for assistance. You need to observe each learner and try to identify the symptoms of learners who are struggling. This is also combined with the need not to interfere too early since it is a natural part of learning to use ICT to have to overcome problems. However, it can be very demoralising to be left too long with a challenge the learner simply cannot see a way round. You need to observe each learner and monitor their progress so that you can quickly identify those who need help. This is not an exact science and you will get it wrong, but asking a person how things are going or saying that many people find this task difficult will do little harm. It is much more damaging for them to feel ignored. During a course you will begin to identify those learners who find ICT difficult and can focus more on identifying when support is needed.

Identifying when a problem is being encountered is essentially fire fighting, but there is another part to supporting learners. This is about ensuring that they are making progress towards the objectives of the programme. This involves the regular review of each individual. You need to plan so that you know what is being achieved. There is a variety of ways of undertaking a review, but in an ICT workshop environment it is probably appropriate to monitor progress against each activity being undertaken and to record what has been achieved. This should be combined with discussions with each learner so that you can build up a picture of their growth. This can easily be combined with feedback about their efforts with particular tasks.

## Role of volunteers

In voluntary and community based settings volunteers are often available to provide extra support in addition to the tutor. They are frequently graduates of earlier programmes so they have some understanding of the course but clearly understand how the individuals feel since they have previous direct experience. The key to using volunteers effectively is to brief them about their role so that they:

- understand their role;
- know what is expected from them and when to refer issues to the tutor;
- have a specific area of responsibility — perhaps they help particular learners;

Volunteers need to be managed in order for them to play a useful role.

## Information, advice and guidance for learners

Many projects and research programmes have highlighted the need for effective information advice and guidance for learners of all ages. Many people who drop out of one type of ICT course often enrol in another because they were unaware of the nature and content of the first one until they had partly completed it. This is a real waste of resources and can be damaging to the confidence and self-esteem of the learners.

Information, advice and guidance need to be provided before a person joins an education or training programme. However, the tutor does have a role whereby early in the course (e.g. first session) they should offer a detailed overview so that any misunderstandings can be immediately identified. Learners may want to progress to other courses. The tutor will often be asked for help in where they should go. It is important to be able to provide clear signposts to other services, information on other ICT courses and referrals to specialist help.

## Personalisation

Personalisation is a term that is being used to describe methods and approaches that allow educational providers and practitioners to customise their provision to meet the needs of learners. It is essentially about trying to develop structures that will be able to meet learners' needs, and placing them at the centre of the system. It could be considered as creating a learner-centred system or culture.

Some characteristics of those who have benefited from a personalised system are independent learners who are able to express their needs and negotiate their learning experiences. They are able to make informed decisions and set personal objectives. In terms of ICT learners' experience, you may want to consider how to:

- help learners become independent users/learners, able to cope with a dynamic subject;
- offer a purposeful experience to meet learners' needs;
- gather feedback from individuals and the whole group of learners;
- customise the course to respond to learners' feedback and objectives.

## Support:

# a summary of key points

— *Support is often the critical difference between a learner completing a course and dropping out. It can take several forms and often the most effective approach is a mix of formal and informal methods.*

— *Problem-solving is a natural part of learning ICT user skills. It is important to allow learners to solve their own problems and only assist when there is a risk of frustration. This must be treated as a learning opportunity and not simply solving the problem. Ask the learner to carry out the solution while you offer advice – do not do it for them.*

— *Observation is an effective way of identifying learners who need help and can overcome some of the difficulty of learners being reluctant to ask for help.*

— *Every difficulty is an opportunity for learning.*

— *Many learners want to practise between sessions, so prepare materials to help and support them.*

— *Create an environment in which it is natural for peers to help each other.*

— *Mentoring and coaching are important ways of helping learners apply their learning in the workplace.*

— *There are many forms of assistive technology to assist students with disabilities.*

— *Approximately ten per cent of the population is left-handed.*

— *Individual support is probably what most learners need, and can be provided through careful organisation and planning of the programme.*

— *Tutor support is often identified by learners as the most valued aspect of a course.*

— *Volunteers and other support staff can play a key role in helping people to learn ICT user skills. The important step is to ensure that they are adequately briefed and understand their role.*

— *Information, advice and guidance need to be available for all learners.*

— *Personalisation is concerned with the customisation of programmes to meet the learners' needs. In a sense it is about a more learner-centred approach.*

# 8 METHODS: TEACHING AND LEARNING TECHNIQUES

## Introduction

ICT is a dynamic subject in which applications change continuously, so learning needs to equip learners with the skills to cope with change and transfer learning to new situations. The consequences of simply helping users to be able to use a narrow range of applications are that, faced with a new challenge, they may well fail. This can have critical effects on the learners' self-esteem and confidence with technology. It can produce users who are dependent on others and easily deterred from using technology.

The ICT Skill for Life standard at level 1 requires that learners become independent users of technology. This is not a simple step but involves assisting them to become confident, able to engage with ICT and develop a structural understanding. The latter involves understanding the underpinning principles that support ICT systems and applications.

The characteristics of independent users and learners of ICT are complex and can be expressed in many ways. The list below is one way of illustrating the characteristics:

- confidence – understand their abilities, knowledge and skills;
- determination/patience;
- positive attitude to computers;
- enthusiasm and motivation;
- ability to transfer skills and knowledge to new situations;
- ability to solve problems;
- willingness to explore, test and investigate;
- understanding of underpinning principles (i.e. structural understanding).

## Experiential learning

Information and communication technology is a practical subject in which many skills and techniques need to be gained. This has led naturally to an emphasis on practice and a focus on undertaking a series of tasks to develop experience. This experiential learning approach has been modelled by Kolb (1984). Figure 17 shows the four-stage model. The four stages are:

- concrete experience;
- observation and reflective observation;
- abstract conceptualisation;
- active experimentation.

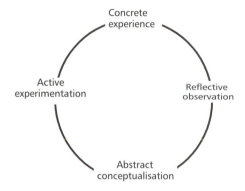

Fig. 17 Kolb Experiential learning model

A learner can join the cycle at any point, but for meaningful learning to occur a full circuit must be completed. The four steps involve carrying out an action, reflecting on the experience, considering the principles underpinning the experience and transferring the understanding to a new situation. Within an ICT workshop it is vital that learners have the opportunity to experience all four steps. Learners will have steps they prefer and others that they are reluctant to participate in. Some will enjoy reflecting on their experiences while others will prefer exploring new situations.

ICT is often seen as an essentially practical subject in which doing is the primary focus. This is correct, but simply doing without the other steps will result in learners who do not understand what they have memorised and are unable to cope with even modest changes. It is perfectly possible to relate ICT methods to the cycle.

## Examples

1. **Experience – left and right mouse buttons produce reactions when clicked.**
2. **Reflection – on reflection, the left and right keys produce different types of actions.**
3. **Conceptualisation – the left button allows you to select objects, position the cursor and move objects, while the right button is related to opening up menus of choices.**
4. **Experimentation – test these conclusions of the role of the different buttons by exploring them in a variety of situations.**

This example shows that a simple experience can lead to learners developing a level of understanding that they can transfer to new situations. In a dynamic subject like ICT, this is vital to produce people who can adapt to changes.

## Active learning

Learning is not a passive process. It involves learners in active participation and this does not simply mean doing exercises. It requires them to be engaged in meaningful, purposeful and understood activities. Learners need to participate in the course. They should not have to spend long periods listening, but should be given every opportunity to discuss, question and challenge assumptions. A small step might be to allow them to select exercises rather than your allocating them. They obviously need to be informed in order to do this effectively so you must ensure exercises are presented in a way that helps selection (e.g. learning objectives explaining what they will be able to do after the successful completion of the task). This could be enhanced by the learner identifying a project to undertake which is relevant to their needs, or working with the tutor to agree tasks.

For learners to be actively involved, they must be fully engaged in analysis, synthesis, and evaluation of their tasks and learning. It is therefore a combination of doing and reflecting on the activity. This could involve them in reviewing their efforts, comparing experiences with other learners, asking questions and considering their work with other experiences they have had. Later in this chapter we will consider a range of methods, many of which promote active learning or could form part of an active learning approach.

## Techniques and methods

There is a wide range of teaching and learning methods that can be used in ICT. A common criticism of the ICT classroom is that too narrow a range of approaches appears to be used. This is a major weakness since, by limiting methods, you will not address many learners' preferred learning styles which may lead to more dropping out and also may fail to produce a full cycle of learning as described by Kolb (1984). Tutors often feel limited by the requirements of specific qualifications or the funding available for the course. However, many methods do not need more time and frequently assist with motivating learners, leading to higher retention and achievement rates.

Currently many ICT user courses are based on individual learning, using work sheets or standard textbooks aided by occasional group work. Worksheets are often criticised, but they can be effectively employed in many situations. Nevertheless, they should not be the only method used and engaging courses are often characterised by a mix of methods. Some learners are interested enough to work at home or use drop-in facilities between sessions, so it is important to consider how to assist this activity. It is equally important to consider those learners who are unable to practise between sessions. A two- or three-hour session once a week for learners unable to practice probably means you will need to review previous work regularly to refresh memories. All courses need to take advantage of a major asset – the other learners. People can help each other if given the opportunity to assist.

Several surveys of ICT courses have shown that learners regard the tutor as the major factor in their learning. They value good tutors above all other resources, so ensure that the learners gain access to you.

Some methods that can be used are:

| | | | |
|---|---|---|---|
| 1. | Group discussion. | 13. | Lecture. |
| 2. | Case studies. | 14. | Workshop. |
| 3. | Problem solving. | 15. | Worksheets. |
| 4. | Simulations. | 16. | Self-directed open learning/CBT |
| 5. | Peer support. | | (computer-based training). |
| 6. | Quizzes. | 17. | Learning diaries. |
| 7. | Buzz groups. | 18. | Feedback from and to learners. |
| 8. | Demonstration. | 19. | Learning from mistakes. |
| 9. | Question and answer. | 20. | Mentoring. |
| 10. | Ice breakers. | 21. | Family learning. |
| 11. | Field trip. | 22. | Review. |
| 12. | One-to-one. | | |

Figure 18 shows the relationship between these methods and the different stages of the cycle. In some cases methods can serve a number of stages, depending on how they are employed.

| Methods | Experience | Reflection | Conceptualisation | Experimenting |
|---|---|---|---|---|
| Group discussion | | | Yes | |
| Case studies | | Yes | Yes | |
| Problem solving | Yes | | | Yes |
| Simulations | Yes | | | Yes |
| Peer support | Yes | Yes | Yes | Yes |
| Quizzes | Yes | | | |
| Buzz groups | | Yes | Yes | |
| Demonstration | Yes | | | |
| Question and answer | Yes | | | |
| Ice breakers | Yes | | | |
| Field trip | Yes | | | |
| One to one | Yes | Yes | Yes | Yes |
| Lecture | Yes | | | |
| Workshop | Yes | | | Yes |
| Work sheets | Yes | | | Yes |
| Self directed open learning/CBT | Yes | Yes | Yes | Yes |
| Learning diaries | | Yes | Yes | |
| Feedback from and to learners | | Yes | Yes | |
| Learning from mistakes | Yes | | | Yes |
| Mentoring | | Yes | Yes | |
| Family learning | Yes | Yes | Yes | Yes |
| Review | | | Yes | |

Fig. 18 Methods and the Kolb cycle

## Group discussion

Group discussions are an important way of allowing individuals to benefit from the experience of a whole group of people. They are widely used in education and training, but often neglected in ICT courses probably due to the emphasis on individual learning methods. ICT is a complex subject with many details to be understood and experienced, and it is therefore normal for individuals to become confused, fail to understand or simply misunderstand. A group discussion allows learners to test their knowledge in a non-threatening environment. It is always easier to ask a peer than to ask the tutor.

Groups provide a change of pace and a more social atmosphere than working alone in front of the computer. Many adults enjoy the company and interaction with other people and may become de-motivated by little or no social interchange. There are many aspects of ICT that are not simply about acquiring technical skills and knowledge. Some possible group discussion topics are:

- Why should you protect your computer against viruses and spyware?
- How safe is it to purchase goods online?
- What are the main health and safety issues involved with using a computer?
- How do you design an interesting website?
- How do you safeguard your information?
- What personal information can people hold about you?

An effective group discussion provides a topic that a small number of people can talk about to produce a reasonable answer. Each member of the group should be able to contribute, thus gaining confidence while learning some new content. It is important that the groups report to the whole class but not in a way that takes too long. You can sometimes bore everyone if the feedback takes longer than the discussion. You might ask each group to write up their conclusions on a chart that you can display. Everyone can then read each other's views and you might allow them to annotate them with post-it note comments.

There are a number of variations on discussion groups but one approach often used is:

- divide the class into small groups (e.g. three or four people);
- present them with a written topic and instructions (e.g. discuss for 15 minutes and record your conclusions on the chart);
- allow everyone five minutes to read charts and add comments;
- highlight some key points and fill in any gaps;
- questions – always allow learners to ask about anything that occurs to them.

There is no need to use discussion groups excessively. Probably no more than one every other session is sufficient. They should be short and intense rather than drawn out.

## Problem solving

The use of ICT has sometimes been described as a process of solving a series of problems. This reflects the nature of the complex discipline in which applications offer an enormous range of functionality, meaning that it is unlikely that you will remember or even have experience of all of them. There are often many alternative approaches depending on your starting point and ultimate objective. Users need to be able to deal with unfamiliar situations or new challenges without immediately being bewildered. In other words they need to be able to solve problems. It is therefore an appropriate approach to provide learners with tasks that involve them in solving problems. This will help them develop useful approaches to working out solutions, see challenges as a natural part of ICT and improve their self confidence.

You can provide problem-solving tasks to individuals, pairs of learners, small groups or the whole class. In some cases you may use a combination of approaches. You could, for example, provide individual tasks but offer feedback to the whole class.

Some possible problem-solving tasks are:

- add a column or row of numbers to produce a total;
- edit the attached image to remove the people on the right of the picture;
- print the letter on headed notepaper;
- import the spreadsheet into a word processed document.

Almost any task can serve as a focus for problem solving. Select one that is perhaps one step beyond the present level of skills or involves finding an alternative approach. The key is to encourage a systematic, logical approach to finding the solution and discourage simply random trial and error. Learners will sometimes fail, so it is important to provide feedback and demonstrate the correct process to identifying the solution.

## Simulations

There is a wide range of different computer-based learning simulations available, all designed to allow a new user to practise ICT skills in a supportive environment. One of the most straightforward is the mouse simulation, which aims to help beginners master the practical dexterity of using a mouse. They will be asked to position the pointer, click on objects, drag and drop and other mouse skills. Often they are timed or earn points by successfully completing the tasks so that the learners are gaining continuous feedback on their performance. A critical advantage of using a simulation is that a mistake does not have any serious consequences while the real environment may well be affected by errors (e.g. windows are opened and the display changes causing new learners to become confused). Once the basic skills are mastered in the simulator, the learner can progress to the actual application without the danger of small errors distracting them from achieving their goals.

The BBC and the Department of Trade and Industry have produced simulations for new users such as Computers Don't Bite, Webwise, Webwise Plus and IT for All that have been effectively used with many thousands of learners. They allow the basic ICT skills to be developed in a friendly and supportive environment.

# Peer support

People will naturally help each other. It is often easier for learners to ask a colleague when they have a problem than the tutor or, in some cases, if they are both in difficulties, to ask the tutor together. Try to avoid discouraging this normal process. Many ICT workshop environments do limit peer support by the way they are structured. Learners are given no opportunities to get to know their neighbours and are often placed too far apart for easy conversations. Tutors only provide individual exercises and no opportunities are offered for group or paired working.

Tutors need to offer every opportunity to the learners to assist each other. This is often a series of simple steps such as:

- introduce everyone at the start of the course – perhaps providing name cards or badges so people can learn each other's name; calling people by their names is often effective in opening a conversation and achieving mutual support;
- provide some paired and small group activities that require peer support;
- encourage conversations and mutual help – silence is sometimes a sign that peer support is not available.

You will want to use some of the methods sparingly, but peer support should be a feature throughout the whole programme. It is even possible for help to be offered between face-to-face sessions if you establish an e-mail group or simply provide everyone with an e-mail address and the opportunity to access an e-mail account.

# Quizzes

A quiz can serve a number of different purposes. It can:

- help you assess the progress of the group;
- encourage interaction within the group;
- provide an opportunity to discuss topics.

There are several ways of undertaking a quiz. One interesting possibility is to divide the class into teams and ask them to set a quiz for the others. This could involve designing questions to be presented on a large screen, searching the World Wide Web for answers, or making an attractive presentation on paper. You are making the quiz a group activity, allowing for skills to be developed or practised and combining it with some assessment while possibly providing some stimulus for discussion.

The occasional quiz is an interesting experience, but over-used it can become ineffective. It is probably best used only once or twice in a course, unless it is one lasting many months (i.e. a continuous theme throughout the course).

# Buzz groups

A buzz group is a special form of discussion group based on asking for two or three people to consider a question quickly and then respond. It can often be effective as an icebreaker in order to gain the participation and engagement of a class. The name comes from the noise of conversation provoked – there is a buzz around the room.

It is a quick method of gaining some ideas from the class and can often be used to introduce a new topic.

## Example

- *Why do you want to learn about ICT? – A good opening for a first session.*
- *What can you use a spreadsheet for? – A useful opening to introduce the use of spreadsheets.*

Buzz groups can also serve a useful role in quickly assessing the group's overall understanding of a topic.

## Example

- *What are key factors in designing a web page?*
- *What should be included in a set of netiquette rules?*

One final role of buzz groups is simply to generate interactions between learners. In a few minutes, a silent room can be changed into a participative environment. However, like many other methods, it is most effective if used only occasionally.

## Demonstration

Demonstrations are an essential teaching method in ICT courses. In a highly practical subject in which learners need to master a variety of techniques and methods, a demonstration is a powerful way of showing them how to undertake a task. Demonstrations can be one-to-one, small group or whole class. The key factor is that everyone involved can see the detail of actions. Normally, the size of the monitor is the main limiting factor unless a video projector is employed. No more than three learners can watch a demonstration on a monitor, but there is no limitation on the size of the audience that can watch one projected except that caused by the nature and size of the room.

In order to carry out an effective demonstration you need to:

- prepare by systematically breaking down the activity into the steps and associated knowledge;
- provide a detailed handout explaining the activity;
- present the demonstration one step at a time – normally slower than would be required in practice so that learners have time to understand what is happening;
- encourage questions;
- repeat key steps, especially in response to questions or comments from learners;
- repeat steps until learners are confident to attempt the activity.

Demonstrations can also be a means of assessing progress, with learners being asked to show the tutor that they can carry out a task. This is often useful if a learner asks for help in completing a task (e.g. I cannot get this to work). A tutor needs to encourage the learners to work independently, so asking them to carry out the task while you watch lets you identify mistakes or poor practice while still leaving them in control.

## Question and answer

Questions are a key part of all types of learning, allowing learners to fill gaps in their understanding while helping you assess progress and the quality of your instruction. You need to create a climate in which asking questions is a natural part of the course, so from the start of the course encourage participation. Questions should be welcomed at all times, but there is an added advantage of those asked when everyone is listening so that the answer is heard by the whole class. Some learners rarely ask questions but you can ensure that they benefit from questions. Make a point of highlighting key questions (e.g. 'Could everyone stop for a moment? I have just been asked an important question and you could all benefit from hearing the answer').

Some useful tactics are:

- at the start of the course explain the importance of asking questions;
- request questions at every opportunity;
- record questions and provide summaries of frequently asked questions;
- encourage questions (e.g. That's a useful question...).

The tutor can also ask questions of individuals or the whole group. This provides you with the means of assessing problems that learners are encountering (e.g. What problems are you having?) or testing the understanding (e.g. Why is it important to ...?).

## Icebreakers

It is always important with a new course to develop discussion and interaction and to put everyone at ease from the start. Various icebreakers can be employed and some useful ones are:

- divide group into pairs and ask them to talk to each other so that they can later introduce their partner to the whole group;
- using a digital camera, ask each person to photograph another member of the group; these are then printed and annotated to produce brief biographical details (e.g. name, reasons for attending the course etc); the resulting poster is displayed so that people can quickly identify colleagues and their names;
- each person is asked to write on Post-it notes what they want to achieve from the course; these are grouped to provide a basis for discussing the course content;
- each person's pocket or bag contents are scanned and the group then asked to identify each learner from the image.

The key is to have an active task that involves everyone and encourages dialogue and participation.

## Field trip

It may seem odd to suggest field trips as part of a user ICT course but in some cases they are important. Some possible examples are:

- A visit to the college learning centre so that the group is encouraged to practise their skills between sessions. This is especially important for individuals without home computers or access to the Internet.
- A trip to an interesting site so that the group can practise their digital photography skills.
- A visit to view public use of ICT such as the local railway station to see electronic displays, public information systems and purchase of tickets through automated systems. Many adults are not aware of the spread of ICT into everyday life.
- A visit to a modern workplace can be very useful for users who are developing their skills in order to gain employment.
- Virtual field trips to show learners the possibilities of online sites (e.g. shopping trips, auctions, museums, art galleries and government sites). This shows the group some of the wider possibilities of ICT skills.

## One-to-one

A large amount of ICT learning is individual so that the interaction between a tutor and a learner is natural. Learners will expect their tutor to help them. However, you will often be supporting a relatively large group of learners so the time available for each person will be limited. It is therefore important to maximise the impact of one-to-one tuition. There are several different one-to-one situations such as:

- helping the learners overcome a problem;
- reviewing progress;
- questions from and to the learner;
- providing a new activity (e.g. new worksheet).

In order to make the most of each interaction it is important that you are aware of the learner, so you need to keep records of their progress, initial assessment and needs.

## Lecture

The lecture is often criticised as a poor teaching method, though this is often because it is poorly employed. It has several important advantages, such as a relatively large volume of material can be presented to the whole class in a short time. The main problems are that it requires the individual members of the group to concentrate on what you say and it is difficult to be certain that everyone has understood.

The key factors to an effective lecture are:

- keep it short (i.e. no longer than 20 minutes);
- provide notes of the lecture's contents so that learners can add comments to them;
- encourage questions so some interaction forms part of the lecture;
- use visual aids because these add impact and offer alternatives to speech alone explaining the topics;
- do not over-use (i.e. no more than once each session);
- incorporate/integrate other methods such as buzz groups within the presentation;
- use them when it is important that everyone hears the same input and answers to questions.

## Workshop

The workshop is probably the main method used in ICT User skills. An effective workshop requires organisation and a blend of methods. It is not simply about offering learners the opportunity to use a computer, but about creating a learning and supportive environment. This involves offering learners opportunities that are meaningful and purposeful. Each workshop session should be structured to maximise learning opportunities. Some useful things to consider are:

- brief learners so they understand the activities they are undertaking;
- activities should be selected to provide the learners with purposeful experience that relates to their objectives;
- peer support is encouraged;
- layout of the room supports co-operation;
- support is always available;
- learners can work at their own pace.

## Worksheets

Worksheets are the means of offering learners a distinct activity with clear objectives which assist them to develop their skills and knowledge. A useful worksheet provides:

- clear objectives;
- opportunity to extend skills and knowledge;
- support to help learners;
- links with the course objective.

Figure 19 illustrates a worksheet. The degree of detail provided for the learner will vary. In this example there is a minimum of detail, which suggests that it is intended for more advanced learners who have previously used the application and have achieved skills in file management. Figure 20 shows a worksheet with the same objectives, but aimed at learners who are still developing their skills in the application and file management. Illustrations play an important role in worksheets especially those intended for new users. They will save a considerable amount of explanation. It is important to check that you are not infringing the copyright of the application owners. Many company Websites provide guidance on the use of screen captures for educational and other purposes.

---

**Worksheet example (based on CLAIT 2006, Alan Clarke)**

**Objectives**

At the end of this activity you will be able to:

1. Import an image from a file.
2. Crop image to improve appearance.
3. Position image on page.
4. Save your new image.

**Resources**

Image files are all stored in drive F: in directory F:\Images

Water.jpg
Ships.jpg
Swans.jpg

**Actions**

1. Open CorelDRAW.

2. Select the New Graphics icon.

3. Select the File menu and Import option. Identify the folder in which the images are stored and use the preview facility to review the images.

4. Select the picture and crop it.

5. Position the image on the page.

6. Print the new image and retain.

7. Save your new image.

8. Close the application.

**Assessment**

Show printout to your colleague and compare results.

---

Fig. 19 Worksheet example – advanced learners

**Worksheet example (based on CLAIT 2006, Alan Clarke)**

**Objectives**

At the end of this activity you will be able to:

1. Import an image from a file.
2. Crop image to improve appearance.
3. Position image on page.
4. Save your new image.

**Resources**

Image files are all stored in drive F: in directory F:\Images

Water.jpg
Ships.jpg
Swans.jpg

**Actions**

1. Open CorelDRAW by selecting the Start button, highlighting Programs and clicking on the CorelDRAW item or by double clicking on the CorelDRAW icon on the Windows desktop.

2. Select the New Graphics icon.

3. Select the File menu and Import option to reveal the Import window. Identify the folder in which the images are stored and use the preview facility to review the images. Select Crop options and double click on the picture's file name. The image will appear in the Crop window.

4. Use the enclosure handles to crop the chosen image. Figure A shows before and after cropping. You can use the handles for large crops and then Select area to crop for precise detail.

Before        After

**Figure A  Cropping**

5. When you are ready, click on the OK button and the positioning pointer will appear on the document for you to position the image precisely. Locate the picture in the centre, but in the top half of the page, and click. The image of the water feature or your own picture will be placed on the document. In some cases the image will be larger than the page and you will need to use the handles to resize the picture to fit the page.

6. Figure B shows the image on the document.

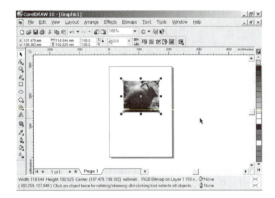

Figure B Image

7. By clicking on the centre handle you will see the handles change shape. If you place your mouse pointer on these handles it too will change shape (i.e. a partial circle with arrows on each end or parallel arrows facing opposite directions). The partial circle will allow you to rotate the image while the parallel arrows let you to skew the image. Experiment with the two pointers by holding down the mouse button to move the image.

8. Skew the image. Turn it upside down and at right angles (Figure C).

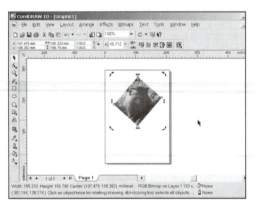

Figure C Skewed Image

9. Save the image by selecting the File menu and the Save option. This will reveal the Save Drawing window. You need to decide where you will save your image. This is done by clicking on the down arrow near the Save in box. This will reveal a list of options. Select floppy disk and insert a disk into the drive. Click in the File name box and enter Imported Image. Click on the Save button. Your image is now saved as the file Imported Image.

10. Close the application either by selecting the File menu and the Exit option or by clicking on the close button in the top right-hand corner of the window.

Fig. 20 Worksheet example – new learners

# Self-directed

It is very common to provide learners with worksheets, books and computer-based learning materials to help them to learn ICT skills at their own pace and in some cases at a time of their choosing. However, to gain the maximum benefit from self-directed study requires good support and is often best suited to being integrated with more conventional approaches. This is often called blended learning. Some key factors in providing effective self-directed learning are:

- self-study materials are carefully evaluated to assess their usefulness;
- support is vital so that no learner has to wait more than a few minutes for assistance when requested;
- support should be proactive so that learners do not always need to ask for help;
- self-study materials are integrated with conventional approaches (e.g. assessment, review, demonstrations etc.).

Self-directed learning can be very effective and popular with some learners, but some will find it ineffective; it tends to suit individuals who have well-developed learning skills and a prior record of education or training achievement.

# Learning diaries

The dynamic nature of ICT makes it essential that learners are able to become independent users, able to transfer their knowledge and experience to new settings, explore new applications and have confidence in themselves as effective learners. Essentially they must be able to cope with change. Many adults have limited confidence in their abilities to learn. A learning diary is a means of helping learners to gain confidence through becoming aware of what they are learning and developing their ability to reflect on experience.

Learning diaries can take a variety of forms and there is no particularly right way of presenting them. They are simply a record of what the learner has experienced and how they feel about it. It may be appropriate in an ICT course to offer learners an electronic diary. You might ask all learners to spend ten minutes at the end of a session making a record of what they have experienced and then reflecting on their own performance between sessions. This can perhaps be combined with setting themselves goals for the next session.

# Feedback from and to learners

In all forms of learning it is important to know how you are doing. Feedback from the tutor is a vital part of helping learners understand their own progress. It can be as informal as a simple comment while looking over a learner's shoulder when walking around the workshop, or a more formal process after an assessment to help individuals improve their performance. It is often difficult for learners to know if they are doing well or poorly. ICT will be new to them and they will not have experience to compare their efforts against.

Feedback is a two-way process so it is important to provide opportunities for the learners to give you feedback. This again may be relatively informal with a casual conversation about a demonstration, whole-class presentation or other form of input, or it may be formal, employing an evaluation sheet on which the individual is assessing the course. It is important to seek feedback and to act on it.

## Learning from mistakes

Learning from your mistakes is a powerful way of developing your skills and understanding. However, learners need to be able to identify where they went wrong and to see the correct path. If they are left to struggle on their own for too long then they may simply become discouraged. There is a balance to be found between giving people space to explore and experiment (i.e. learning from trial and error) and leaving them without support. There is no exact formula since different people will respond in different ways. Some people like to learn in this way while others do not.

## Mentoring

There are various ways of defining mentoring, but essentially it is concerned with providing a learner with a more experienced peer to assist them. It is widely used in the workplace where more experienced workers act as mentors to new staff. In terms of ICT it would best be seen as a way of adding value to the training or educational programme when the individual learners return to work to use the techniques and applications they have been shown on the course. The mentor is available to assist them. The role varies considerably but could involve helping the learner:

• through their training or educational programme;
• identifying and developing evidence of their competence;
• through advice and guidance when they are making choices;
• transferring their classroom learning to the workplace.

Essom (2003) produced a resource pack for ICT mentors working in the voluntary and community sectors. It provides practical assistance for anyone seeking to develop a mentoring programme with volunteers and demonstrates that mentoring is not simply for the workplace but is also effective with vulnerable learners.

## Family learning

Family learning, as the name suggests, is the involvement of members of a family in a learning activity. It normally means that at least two generations of the family are involved (e.g. parent and child or grandparent and grandchild). Most people learn a great deal within their family about society, behaviour, values, attitudes and responsibilities. It is therefore a natural place for any form of learning. For many parents, an important reason to be able to use ICT is the potential it has to help their children's education. There is a natural connection between ICT and family learning, with the added advantage that many children have grown up with ICT so have considerable confidence in their ability to use it.

Family learning approaches have been used extensively with literacy and numeracy. There is the possibility of embedding ICT in these subjects for a family learning approach. However, learning about ICT in the context of family learning is also widely employed. A guide to ICT and family learning, along with other resources, is available from *www.helpisathand.gov.uk/resources/teaching-learning/family/*.

# Review

It is important to regularly review individual and group progress. Learners need to know how they are doing. It is not easy if you are studying a new subject to judge your own development in isolation. It is easy to believe you are doing poorly or well if there is no comparison. It is important that the group have a context that they understand. This should include:

- overall course objectives;
- individual activity objectives;
- awareness of the speed and level of success that they should be achieving.

Objectives should be provided at the start of the course and presented in a meaningful way. Each activity should relate to them and again should be easy to understand. This enables the individuals to monitor their own progress as they complete each session and individual exercises. Some straightforward steps can be very helpful, such as explaining what you aim to cover in each session and how many exercises they will be expected to undertake.

There are several ways of undertaking a review, such as:

- individual;
- peer;
- group.

You will need to discuss individual progress with each learner regularly, with perhaps a few words on completion of an individual exercise or a longer discussion to review several sessions. The key is that learners are all aware of their progress, that you can judge what assistance they need and can assess your own performance.

Peer review is often very effective in that learners can compare notes about their work.

# Visual aids

ICT is clearly a visual subject in that learners will spend a large part of their courses looking at a display. However, it is important to consider whole-class and group activities. The video or data projector offers the means to demonstrate applications and operating system functions to a large group. The electronic whiteboard again provides the means to assist the teaching and training of ICT. Presentation applications (e.g. Microsoft PowerPoint) offer the way to develop structured presentations.

There are some practical points relating to visual aids that it is important to stress.

- Do not overuse visual aids.

- Straightforward is often better than flashy.
- Check all points in the room to ensure that everyone can see the display. Remember that you may be obscuring the view.

## Webquests

A Webquest is an approach to using the World Wide Web to help people develop good analytical and judgement skills. It can be undertaken individually or in small groups. The learner or group is given an objective which involves the gathering and analysis of information for a purpose. They are provided with a list of Web resources so they do not have to search and locate sources since the emphasis is on judging the information. A key ICT skill is the ability to judge the quality of information that is available on Websites. This is often difficult to develop but the Webquest is a useful way of developing the skill.

The University of California, San Diego developed the approach and has a Webquest resource at *webquest.sdsu.edu/*. This provides help to teachers of any subject seeking to use the method.

# Conclusion

There are many different methods that can be employed in the teaching or training of ICT user skills. The key is to use them appropriately for the learners you are working with and the objective you are trying to achieve. It is poor practice to use too many different methods, but it is equally poor to use too narrow a range. Learners will have different needs and preferences so it is important to employ a mix so that no one is isolated and everyone is included.

## *Methods: teaching and learning techniques:*

# a summary of key points

_____ *ICT is a dynamic subject. It is not enough to be able to use a small range of applications. Learners need to have the confidence and ability to transfer their learning to new situations.*

_____ *Kolb's Experiential Learning Model provides a structure to design the learning experience.*

_____ *Learning is an active process and learners need to participate in a meaning and purposeful way.*

_____ *It is important for the tutor to develop and use a range of teaching and learning techniques that will:*

*– promote and encourage individual learning;*
*– facilitate learning in groups;*
*– facilitate learning through experience;*
*– evaluate its practice.*

## Introduction

Assessment is a normal part of ICT User courses. There is a range of qualifications that learners may be undertaking. However, some adult learners will be studying for the first time in many years and may well have a background of poor academic achievement, which is likely to make them reluctant to take part in tests and become very nervous when faced with an assessment of any type. They will probably have limited learning and assessment skills. An important element in the initial assessment of participants is to judge their experience of learning and assessment, which will enable you to provide them with an understanding of the form that the ICT User qualifications assessment will take. If it is a long time since they last studied, they may have never experienced methods such as portfolios and competency-based approaches.

Tutors can employ a range of methods to assess learners' progress. These include:

- analysing learners' completed assignments;
- listening to learners while they explain to the tutor how to undertake an activity;
- listening to learners while they explain to each other how to undertake an activity;
- observing learners demonstrating how to carry out a specific task;
- general observation of learners undertaking exercises;
- learners' self-assessment;
- peer assessment;
- questionnaires;
- asking learners questions;
- qualifications assessment.

This is a mixture of formal and informal assessment methods. Some are focused on the assessment of skills while others are aimed at testing knowledge. Overall you are trying to assess the outcomes of learning and learners' achievements, using appropriate methods in order to make use of information. There are many purposes of assessment such as:

- an external qualification;
- an internal standard (i.e. within an organisation);
- personal achievement.

You can integrate assessment in normal activities rather than separate it as a special event. This will reduce learner stress. It is also an efficient use of time, but the assessment conditions of some qualifications will limit your freedom of choice and you need to consider them when planning your course.

The Qualification and Curriculum Authority (QCA, 2006a) has developed ten principles for assessment for learning. These make a strong case for relating assessment to the learning process. The principles make connections between assessment and:

- planning;
- how learners learn;
- teaching methods;
- teachers' skills;
- motivation;
- standards and learning objectives;
- feedback;
- self-assessment.

## Learning objectives

Assessment cannot operate in a vacuum, but needs to relate to specific learning aims and objectives which allow you to make judgements and to offer feedback. In particular learner feedback needs to be based on a shared understanding of the objectives and the criteria used to judge them. It is vital that learners understand what they are trying to achieve. This helps them to benefit from feedback, develop the ability to assess their own efforts and become independent ICT users.

One useful way of assisting learners to understand the objectives they are working towards is to express them in terms that are practical and relate to what they will be able to do.

## *Example*

*After successfully completing this module the learners will be able to:*

- *enter text and numbers;*
- *correct their own errors;*
- *present their text and numbers using different fonts, character sizes and alignment.*

At all stages of the course it is important to explain the objectives of the activities and how they will be assessed.

# Formative and summative assessment

There are two broad approaches to assessment:

- formative;
- summative.

Formative assessment is intended to gather information to provide feedback on the students' progress so that gaps in their understanding and skills can be identified and remedied. Essentially, all assessment after the initial identification of needs and skills is formative until the final assessment at the end of the course.

Summative assessment is the final part of a course. It is often linked to the qualification being studied. It is the judgement of the skills and knowledge learnt during the course and is often decided by using an external test. The success of the course for the individual is often shown by the summative assessment.

## Recognising and recording progress and achievement in non-accredited learning

Many ICT courses are not accredited to a specific qualification. However, the Department for Education and Skills along with the Learning and Skills Council, Ofsted and Adult Learning Inspectorate have been developing an approach to recognising and recording progress and achievement in these courses and programmes (Learning Skills Council, 2005).

The recognising and recording progress and achievement in non-accredited learning (RARPA) approach is a systematic one and consists of:

- establishing course aims which are appropriate for learners;
- undertaking initial assessment;
- identifying individual learning objectives;
- formative assessment;
- learner self-assessment combined with tutor summative assessment.

RARPA is evidence-based, but allows you to employ a wide range of methods that are suitable for your context and learners. Some of the possible methods are self, group and peer assessments, individual learner records, learning diaries, portfolios of work and outcomes of exercises.

## Portfolios

A portfolio is a collection of evidence to demonstrate that an individual is competent in a range of tasks. They have been employed in arts and crafts for many years since an essential part of demonstrating your capability are examples of work undertaken. They are now widely used in relation to National Vocational Qualifications (NVQs) which are aimed at accrediting the competence of an individual in a vocational subject. They can take a variety of forms, but the evidence is defined by the awarding body. It is often related to showing that skills and knowledge can be applied in a work context (e.g. examples of business letters word processed). Portfolios are also the means of providing evidence to illustrate existing skills and knowledge as part of a process of accrediting prior learning.

A variety of types of evidence may be included in a portfolio, such as:

- observation of the learner undertaking a task;
- screen captures;
- witness statements;
- photographs (e.g. showing learning carrying out tasks);
- products (e.g. web pages designed by learners for their employer).

Portfolios are a way of reducing the burden of tests and examinations on learners and showing that they have the practical skills and understanding to undertake tasks.

## E-portfolio

In simple terms, an e-portfolio is a natural extension of the conventional portfolio, but this would be a very limited view of its possibilities. It can offer the learners the possibility of:

- storing their achievements and objectives;
- recording their exercises, assignments and other learning outcomes;
- reflecting on their learning;
- keeping evidence from informal learning events;
- presenting their achievements in a variety of ways (e.g. curriculum vitae);
- providing a lifelong record of achievement.

There is considerable interest in the use and development of e-portfolios, but experience is still limited and in many ways their potential has not yet been realised. The British Educational and Communication and Technology Agency (Becta, 2006) has recently discussed the nature of e-portfolios and suggests that they may take a range of forms from a personal, relatively informal record to a highly structured system. There may be a range of e-portfolios to serve different contexts (e.g. personal and employment).

The outcomes of ICT courses are often electronic so that storing and manipulating them in an e-portfolio seems a natural process, with the added advantage that using them can be integrated into the learning activities.

## Peer assessment

Peer assessment involves learners commenting on or judging the work of the others. It is often used as part of formative processes in offering an alternative viewpoint to that of the tutor. It can also contribute to summative assessment although this is rarer in ICT user programmes. Peer assessment is one of the means of encouraging learners to become more independent. Its main weakness is that learners are not as aware of standards or comparisons as the tutor, so they can be either too critical or too complimentary. There is always a need for some type of tutor moderation of peer assessment.

In ICT user courses, peer assessment can play a useful role in providing feedback to learners on their work so that they gain a range of views. If this is done in a controlled, empathic way it can be very supportive.

## Example

1. *A learner demonstrates how to carry out a task to a small group of other students. They are then asked to comment before taking their turn.*
2. *Each learner's work is assessed for quality by his or her peers (e.g. quality of editing a digital image).*

Peer assessment can significantly increase the feedback to learners on their work, but it should not replace it. Learners place great value on their tutor's feedback.

## Self-assessment

Learners should be encouraged to assess their own work, as this helps them to develop an understanding of the quality of work expected of them and to become independent users of ICT. At its simplest, the tutor should always ask the learners for their own judgement of what they have achieved.

## Example

- *How difficult did you find the exercise?*
- *What problems did you encounter?*
- *How useful is this activity in your job?*
- *The learner will often be aware of issues that this type of self-assessment will reveal so that you can assist them to improve.*

A more sophisticated form of self-assessment is to provide the learner with some form of marking scheme so they can mark their own work. It can also form part of peer assessment if pairs of learners mark each other's work. This is normally part of the formative process, letting learners gain more objective insight into their work and allowing more feedback to be available to them. In this case the feedback is from themselves or a colleague.

## Online assessment

The use of online assessment is growing rapidly and has been employed extensively in some subject areas including IT Key Skills. A large element of the growth has been in the use of multi-choice type questions presented online to the learners. It is often popular with students since the marking is automated and immediate in some cases. Government policy is likely to encourage this rapid expansion of online or e-assessment to continue.

E-skills passport is a self-assessment online system to help you judge the level of your skills (Figure 21). It allows specific ICT user skills for individual jobs to be profiled so learners can judge what skills they need to develop. Figure 22 shows part of the bksb's (West Nottinghamshire College) system to assess ICT basic skills.

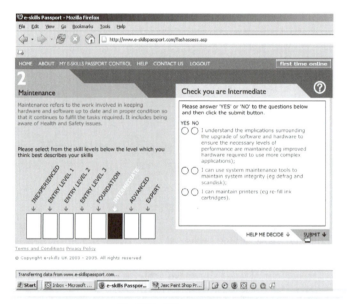

Fig. 21 E-skills passport

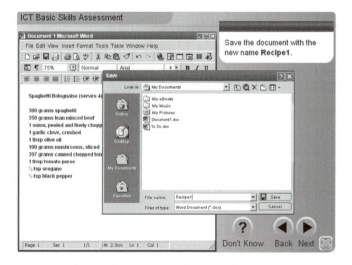

Fig. 22 ICT Basic Skills Assessment bksb (West Nottinghamshire College)

The government's e-learning policy, Harnessing Technology, has the priority of providing 'integrated online personal support for learners' (DfES, 2005a). This will almost certainly encourage all forms of e-assessment and e-portfolios. This is reinforced by the policy of the Qualifications and Curriculum Authority which aims to have e-assessment as part of all new qualifications by 2009 and for all awarding bodies to employ e-portfolios by 2009 (QCA, 2006b).

## Checklists

One straightforward assessment method is the checklist. It may be a guide to markers identifying the key areas that need to be included in the assignment, assistance for a tutor on what to look for during observation, or an aid for learners on how to judge their own work. In all forms it is often a list of issues, points or steps that are relevant and aims to ensure that all the key points are covered. Figure 23 provides an example of a checklist.

| Key points | Notes |
|---|---|
| 1. Spelling or grammatical errors | 1. Would the use of the spelling or grammar checkers have identified the mistake? |
| 2. Margins | 2. Are the margins correct? |
| 3. Page orientation | 3. Is the page orientated correctly? |
| 4. Text | 4. Has all the set text been entered? |
| 5. Formatting instructions<br>    - font<br>    - character size<br>    - line spacing | 5. Have all the instructions been followed correctly? |
| 6. Amendments | 6. Have all the changes been successfully made? |
| 7. Image | 7. Has the image been inserted correctly? |
| 8. Header and footer | 8. Has the header been used to identify the learner and centre? |

Fig. 23 Marking checklist

## Project/assignment

A widely employed approach to summative assessment is the project or assignment, consisting of a set of activities for the learner to undertake in a set period of time. The evidence is the finished assignment. They can be designed by the awarding body, educational provider or even the learner (e.g. work-based project). In all cases they aim to assess the content of the course being undertaken. Many awarding bodies publish example assignments to demonstrate to tutors what will be required. They can be very helpful since they allow you to design your own and assist you with preparing your learners.

## Example

*Develop a spreadsheet to analyse the sales of a product over a 12 month period.*

*The spreadsheet should include:*

- *the use of standard functions;*
- *developing formulæ;*
- *linking two or more sheets together;*
- *effective presentation of results (i.e. use of formatting options).*

## Questionnaires

Probably the most used form of assessment or test is the questionnaire. Although there are several types, multiple choice questionnaires are probably the most frequently used. These ask the learner to select from alternative answers. It is easy to use and mark, but is limited to testing the knowledge of the learners rather than their skills.

## Example

*What is RAM?*

*1. Random access memory.*
*2. Rich area memory.*
*3. Radio active monitor.*

The example demonstrates one way of presenting a multiple choice with all the options visible. An alternative is hidden multiple choice where only one answer at a time is revealed. This is a more challenging approach wherein learners are unable to compare the alternatives and work out the correct answer.

There are several ways of presenting a multiple choice questionnaire such as:

- individual exercise using paper presentation;
- individual exercise using an on-screen display;
- group or whole-class exercise using projected questions;
- oral questions with the whole class (i.e. individual answers);
- oral questions with small groups.

You need to select the way that fits the purpose. A whole-class or group exercise will encourage participation and allow you to gain a view of the overall level, while an individual exercise is essentially about assessing each person.

Other forms of questionnaire are:

- **Short answer questions** – these require learners to write a few sentences to show their understanding. This allows you to probe the knowledge of students in more depth than multiple-choice questions.
- **True or false questions** – essentially asking the learners to select from two opposites.
- **Filling gaps** – learners are asked to complete sentences by filling in the blanks.

## Feedback

The purpose of assessment is to analyse the performance of learners against some type of criteria, often with the aim of improving their performance. It is therefore essential to provide the learners with some useful feedback. It is helpful to know that they have been given a mark of seven out of a possible ten, but much more useful to also be told the average mark for the group is six since this enables them to judge their performance in the context of their peers.

Consider how to add value to the assessment result with feedback. You might want to provide:

- average marks of the group or of previous groups;
- identification of strengths and weaknesses;
- annotations on assignments so that learners' attention is drawn to key points, both good and poor;
- suggestions for further work.

Assessment results can also provide the tutor with useful feedback about what worked well and what needs improving. Poor results in specific areas will identify aspects to investigate. They may simply be more difficult or may show that your approach is flawed.

## Evaluation

It is important to evaluate your own programmes. As there is a variety of ways of carrying out an evaluation, it is often useful to combine different approaches so that a balanced view is achieved. You might bring together:

- results of the individual assessments (e.g. qualifications achieved);
- drop outs from the course;
- evaluation forms;
- verbal views of the learners.

There are different levels of evaluation. The Kirkpatrick Evaluation Model (Kirkpatrick, 1998) is based on four levels:

- Level 1 – reaction;
- Level 2 – learning;

- Level 3 – behaviour;
- Level 4 – results.

**Level 1** is concerned with how the learners reacted to the course. In simple terms, did they enjoy the process? This could be measured by simply giving them a feedback form at the end of the course with questions such as:

- What did you like about the course?
- What did you dislike?

**Level 2** is concerned with how much the learners developed during the course. What skills and knowledge did they gain? This can be measured in a variety of way such as:

- assignments;
- exercises;
- observation;
- self-assessment;
- summative assessments for qualifications.

**Level 3** is concerned with measuring the learners' change in behaviour. In the context of ICT User Skills this may be linked to developing confidence, self-esteem and a positive attitude to ICT. It can be difficult to measure changes in behaviour over a short programme, but some possible ways are:

- peer assessment;
- tutor-learners' reviews;
- observation;
- self-assessment.

**Level 4** is concerned with the outcomes of the course. It is often related to training programmes within an organisation in which you are seeking to identify if the training produced increased productivity or similar outcomes. It is possible to measure this effect if you are carrying out ICT User Skills within an organisation, but if the course is general and intended for individuals, it is more difficult to measure. Some possible methods to identify impact are:

- follow-up questionnaires after the end of the course;
- interviews with returning learners who have enrolled on more advanced courses;
- appraisals of employers on in-house courses.

Kirkpatrick stresses that the four levels are a whole and should not be considered in isolation from each other.

As part of the course planning, consider how you intend to evaluate the programme and build in the means throughout the course, with the aim of considering all four levels of the Kirkpatrick model.

## Assessment:

# a summary of key points

——— *Assessment is a part of a majority of ICT courses. There are several ICT User qualifications that are undertaken by thousands of learners each year.*

——— *It is important that assessment relates closely to the programme's learning objectives.*

——— *There are two main aspects to assessment. They are formative and summative assessment. Summative is often the subject of considerable discussion since it relates to the achievement of a qualification. However, formative must not be neglected since it can contribute to the quality of the learning experience.*

——— *Recognising and Recording Progress and Achievement in Non-accredited Learning (RARPA) is an approach to gathering evidence in non-accredited courses.*

——— *Portfolios of evidence have been extensively employed (e.g. NVQs) as a means of assessing performance without the need for a test or examination.*

——— *There is considerable interest around the world in developing e-portfolios which would allow an individual to collect evidence of their achievements throughout their lives.*

——— *Peer assessment can play a useful role in providing feedback to learners.*

——— *Self-assessment is a learning skill that everyone needs, so learners should be encouraged to develop a critical and balanced view of their own efforts.*

——— *Online assessment is growing rapidly and is often popular with students.*

——— *The checklist can often play a useful role in other forms of assessment (e.g. self assessment) and has the virtue of being straightforward and low cost.*

——— *Projects/assignments are ways of offering the learner the opportunity to be assessed in a context appropriate to them.*

——— *Questionnaires are useful when assessing a large group of learners, but limited in their depth.*

——— *All forms of assessment should lead to feedback to the learner.*

——— *Evaluation should be a part of all courses and learning programmes.*

# 10 CONTINUOUS PROFESSIONAL DEVELOPMENT

## Introduction

We have stressed that ICT is a dynamic subject requiring that learners be able to cope with change and transfer their learning to new situations. For similar reasons tutors must continually seek to keep themselves up to date. They must maintain and enhance their skills and knowledge of a variety of pedagogical, technical and non-technical areas including:

- trends in the use of ICT (e.g. at work, in the home etc);
- new or amended qualifications;
- changes in occupational and other standards;
- pedagogical methods;
- e-government developments;
- changes in hardware (e.g. hand held devices);
- reflecting on and evaluating one's own performance and planning future practice;
- new versions of applications;
- e-learning;
- nature of current learners (e.g. employment);
- government policy in relation to ICT.

Many professions, including organisations such as the Chartered Institute of Personnel and Development (CIPD), Royal College of Nursing and the Law Society, have already established the need for members to undertake Continuous Professional Development to maintain their status. It is therefore a natural step for ICT tutors and trainers to need to undertake continuous professional development (CPD). Some ICT trainers are already likely to be members of the CIPD (Chartered Institute for Personnel and Development).

CIPD requires that its members, who are often training managers and officers, make a continuous effort to develop their skills and knowledge to maintain and extend their professional competency. The emphasis is that development is a key element in being a professional. CIPD suggest a wide range of learning methods including:

- e-learning;
- coaching and mentoring;
- secondments;
- training courses;
- action learning.

# Institute for Learning

The Institute for Learning is the professional body for tutors in post-16 education. One of its key priorities is to develop a CPD process so that members can undertake activities to enhance and maintain their skills and knowledge as professional tutors. The institute has established a portal so that tutors can be informed about CPD developments: (*www.ifl.ac.uk/cpd_portal/cpd_index.html*).

The government policy is that tutors will need a licence to practise in order to teach and can eventually reach Qualified Teacher Status. Achieving and maintaining this status will depend on the production of CPD evidence. It is therefore important to recognise that keeping records of personal development is becoming a vital process. The Institute is currently trialling a CPD approach for tutors and you can find more about it at their portal.

A consultation is being undertaken on a CPD framework to develop e-learning skills, produced by the Learning and Skills Development Agency. This relates closely to the needs of ICT tutors so may be a model for their professional development.

# Barriers to CPD

Individuals are faced with several barriers to undertaking CPD. The two main ones are:

- **time** – fitted into a busy life, developing yourself is difficult and must compete for time with many other aspects of your lifestyle;
- **cost** – in some cases activities will be expensive (e.g. gaining access to the latest versions of applications).

There is also the scale of the challenge in a subject such as ICT, with continuous change a major factor. Meeting the challenge requires careful planning, keeping records and prioritising your efforts. It is probably impossible to be completely up to date with every associated development, but the question to ask is, do you need to be. It is well worth considering your needs and priorities.

# Methods

There is a wide range of possible methods that you can employ to develop your skills and knowledge. In simple terms, anything that helps you learn could be used. Some possible methods are:

- reading;
- evaluation and feedback;
- appraisal;
- observation;
- peer assessment;
- courses;

- developing materials;
- work experience;
- learners;
- new applications.

It is important that you are aware of your needs and systematically use your learning opportunities to address them.

## Reading

A massive amount of information is published about ICT developments. There are many sources, from national newspapers to specialist online newsletters (e.g. e-skills UK). These serve different purposes and you must decide what you need. A newspaper will often illustrate changes and new trends so can help you identify future technical developments for you to find more about. However, they are unlikely to provide details of a technical change and you will need to read a journal or magazine for more depth. Many manufacturers and suppliers offer comprehensive technical information on their Websites.

An approach you might want to consider is to set yourself a series of challenges to read about specific developments. At the top you might envisage a cone, where a national newspaper section of ICT provides the breadth and at the base is the producers' technical material. You are moving from the general to the specific. For this approach to be effective, you need to set yourself objectives.

Many online sources offer the opportunity to agree to receive regular e-mail updates, but you can often be overwhelmed with information. Some sources of reading include:

- ICT sections of newspapers;
- awarding body newsletters;
- online newsletters;
- reference books;
- developers' websites;
- inspection reports;
- research into ICT teaching and e-learning.

## Evaluation and feedback

Earlier we placed some emphasis on tutors evaluating their own work. This is obviously an important aspect when attempting to improve your course. It is also a way of identifying the strengths and weaknesses of your own approach. A clear evaluation will indicate in what areas you need to improve. In a similar way, feedback from learners and the success in achieving the course qualifications (i.e. reasons for failure) or any common weaknesses in learners' performance may indicate professional development needs.

# Appraisal

Many organisations now provide their staff with a regular appraisal which includes assessing their future development needs. This is an opportunity to gain feedback from your manager, which is valuable in that it provides a different perspective on your performance in addition to your own and that of colleagues. It is also a way of recording past development work and future intentions. This is useful in an age where evidence will be needed to prove professional competence.

# Observation

There are two different types of observation that can contribute to your professional development. These are:

- peer observation and feedback of your own performance;
- personal observation of new developments and uses of ICT.

Many education and training providers regularly undertake observations of all their tutors and trainers which is intended to maintain and improve standards. These offer you an important opportunity to see yourself as others see you, to ask for feedback. If your own employer does not undertake observation then ask a colleague to watch you organise your class. It is useful to supply your observer with some key issues to consider, aspects of your performance that you are seeking to improve. Figure 24 gives a simple example of an observation sheet that you might want to use to gain feedback on your presentation skills.

---

**Observation sheet – presentation**

1. Presentation of information

    – Gain attention of learners
    – Maintain interest
    – Clear
    – Technical terms explained
    – Links to curriculum

2. Answers to questions

    – Encouraged
    – Answers used as learning points
    – Clear
    – Technical terms explained

3. Test understanding

    – Questions to learners

4. Links to next steps

---

Fig. 24 Observation sheet presentation

The use of ICT is constantly developing and changing, both because of technical enhancements and the spread of technology in society. This can be very fast and it is important as an ICT user tutor or trainer to be aware of the latest developments. An effective way is simply to look around you as you participate in society and consider what people are doing with technology.

- How are people communicating (e.g. mobile telephones, text messaging and cameras)?
- How are people gaining access to information (e.g. public information systems in railway stations, shopping centres, banks, government sources and links to other media)?
- What applications are being used in the home, at work and in society?
- How are young people, often the initial adopters of developments, applying technology in new ways and using ICT in their lives?

Observation, in isolation, is unlikely to meet all your needs, but it will help you consider trends and compare what you are reading with what you are seeing. Your own learners can often supply information about trends and overcome stereotypes about the use of ICT made by certain groups.

## Peer support

Observation by a colleague is a major form of peer assessment, providing a useful insight into your performance. It can be extended by identifying a mentor or a coach from your colleagues, who will assist you with advice and guidance. A simple role is to discuss ideas with you so that you have another person's view of developments. A mentor is normally a more experienced person who is offering you their informed view. While it can be a powerful approach to professional development it does require a relationship of mutual trust to be established between yourself and the mentor. To work effectively, mentoring requires openness and honesty.

## Courses and conferences

A course or conference can often assist with professional development in three ways. You can attend one about a technical matter or about improving your teaching or training skills and that is perfectly sensible. A key benefit is that you meet other tutors from different environments who are able to share their experiences with you. Another method is to attend a colleague's course that you also teach so that you can see an alternative approach, often the most difficult thing to identify (i.e. an alternative to your own approach). Obviously this could be combined with observation where you provide your colleague with feedback.

Probably the commonest approach to developing ICT user tutors is to require them to undertake the course that they will be teaching as a learner. This can be useful to as you have first-hand experience of another teacher as well as understanding the impact the course has on learners.

## Developing materials

In order to develop learning materials, a tutor needs to have made a systematic analysis of the topics and probably will have had to undertake the tasks. These activities have the extra benefits of helping you to develop expertise in the area. It is an attractive development method in that you gain useful materials for your work, as well as improving your own skills and knowledge at the same time.

## Work experience

The use of ICT is well established across almost all industries and sectors of the economy. It is also increasingly a useful tool in people's social lives. It is important that ICT tutors are aware of the range of different purposes that ICT is used for. This is made more difficult since the application of ICT is continuously changing and developing. It is therefore imperative that tutors are able to undertake some form of regular work experience to study current use. This does not mean that you need to spend weeks every year in a company working with ICT. What is more likely to be effective are short visits to a wide variety of enterprises. This will provide the breadth of knowledge you need to offer ICT learning in a purposeful way to meet the learners' needs.

## Learners

Your learners are a useful professional development resource. Their aspirations and motivations can inform you about trends within society. The requirements of their employers will keep you informed about how ICT is being used in business.

## New applications

All applications are regularly updated so it is important for the ICT tutor to have the opportunities to explore the latest versions. New products are often reviewed by experts so reading a review can give you an insight into what has changed. However, nothing replaces using a new product so that you can assess it for yourself. An approach that many tutors find useful is to review the new version while amending a worksheet or another exercise so that it can be used with the application. This provides a focus for your examination of the product.

There are many ways of developing yourself. The key to success is preparation. A systematic, logical analysis of your needs combined with a plan to meet your objectives will take you a long way. It will also ensure that your limited time is well spent.

# Self-assessment

A great deal of emphasis is now placed in educational institutions of all types on the ability to self-assess strengths and weaknesses. For the individual tutor or trainer, it is an important skill to be able to judge your own performance, combined with the strengths and weaknesses of your skills and knowledge. This will allow you to identify the areas of your skills and knowledge that need to be improved, updated and studied.

The list below is based on the Adult Learning Inspectorate's advice to its inspectors when conducting lesson observations (Adult Learning Inspectorate, 2005). It has been adapted to provide a range of issues to consider when assessing yourself.

## Reflection list

1.  How effective is your teaching or training?

    Consider how you:

    - prepare your learning programme (e.g. materials, exercise and activities);
    - plan the learning programme;
    - control your class;
    - brief your learners about the programme;
    - employ teaching/training methods;
    - manage time.

2.  How up to date are your skills and knowledge?

    Consider your knowledge of:

    - ICT applications;
    - how technology is used in the workplace;
    - how technology is used in the home.

3.  How well do you motivate learners to learn?

    - Consider your ability to excite and interest learners (e.g. what are your personal retention and achievement rates?).
    - How successful are you at encouraging learners to support each other and contribute to discussions?
    - Are your exercises and activities appropriate for the learners?
    - What methods do you use to engage learners (e.g. group discussions, peer exercises and whole class activities)?

4.  How well can you judge your learners' progress?

    - Are you able to judge the learners' needs?
    - How good are you at assessing learners' work?

5.  How well do you make use of the resources available to you?

    - Equipment (e.g. electronic whiteboards, digital cameras, scanners, video/data projectors and applications).
    - Rooms, text books and other materials.

6.  How often do you reflect on a teaching/training session to analyse how well it went?

If undertaken systematically, this form of reflective self-assessment can help you reach a clear view of your own skills, knowledge and performance. You could take the outcomes and produce your own self-improvement programme.

# Records and evidence

It is important that you keep records of your professional development. This will help in proving your competence, accrediting your prior learning and perhaps in gaining promotions or new posts. Your records are rather like a portfolio of evidence to demonstrate competency as an ICT teacher or trainer. It is likely to cover many years (e.g. lifelong) so it is worth considering how to keep and maintain them. Some professional bodies require evidence that relates to a specific time period (e.g. no more than two years old) and will provide a structure for evidence.

Records need to be:

- Accessible (i.e. employers and professional bodies will want to see them occasionally so their ease of access is important).
- Well presented (i.e. the most comprehensive record will not impress if it is presented as a pile of information without any structure).
- Comprehensive (i.e. the records need to address your needs and the professional requirements of your post).

Evidence needs to be:

- Current (e.g. include recent evidence).
- Assessable (i.e. include self assessments and other forms of assessment – appraisals and qualifications).
- Comprehensive. Some examples of evidence are:
  - examples of work undertaken (e.g. worksheets);
  - minutes of meetings of professional bodies showing contribution;
  - course results;
  - inspection feedback;
  - peer observation feedback.

Almost anything can be evidence, but probably the most useful are things that show your competence, especially if they are provided by independent and acceptable external sources.

Harnessing Technology, the Government's e-learning strategy, aims to offer every citizen the opportunity to have an e-portfolio to maintain their records of achievements. Its form is not finalised, but this may well serve as a secure repository for your CPD evidence.

# Continuous professional development:
## a summary of key points

— Continuous professional development is a part of being an ICT tutor. In a dynamic and rapidly evolving subject there is a continuous need to update your skills and knowledge.

— The requirements for being a tutor in post-16 education will require a positive approach to CPD.

— There are many ways of maintaining and extending professional skills and knowledge. The key is a systematic approach based on addressing your needs.

— The skills of self-assessment are a vital part of CPD. It is important to undertake a structured reflection of your own performance at regular intervals. This may well form the basis for your development plan.

— A part of professional development is the organised acquisition of evidence to demonstrate your skills, knowledge and performance.

# APPENDIX 1: COMMON PROBLEMS FOR NEW ICT USERS

We should not underestimate the potential for ICT systems to confuse new learners. Computer systems have developed numerous conventions and practices that experienced users take for granted, but which can bewilder new users. Also designers of systems do not always follow conventions or standards. Some common problems or sources of confusion are shown below. You may want to compile your own, since this will help you to assist learners overcome them.

## Messages

New users are often confused by the messages that can suddenly appear and which are intended to help them. They can be confronted by questions that they are not sure how to answer such as:

Do you want to save the changes…?

Many new users will not be sure and can be left waiting for help before they can progress.

Microsoft Excel displays a number of error messages that can confuse new users and in some cases experienced ones, for example:

- #REF!
- #NAME?
- #####
- #DIV/0!
- #N/A
- #NUM!
- #VALUE!
- #NULL!

## Language

ICT has lots of new terms that need to be explained such as:

- drives;
- files (e.g. jpeg, gif, txt and xls);
- folder/directories;
- memory stick, pen drive, flash drive and dongle;
- modem/router;

- headers and footers;
- read write.

The potential for confusion is enormous and needs a systematic approach to reduce this.

## Interfaces

Modern GUI interfaces offer considerable choice and flexibility, but for new users learning to undertake specific tasks, the variety of ways to undertake many tasks can be a source of confusion such as:

- Unintentionally minimising a window – new users may assume it has been deleted.
- Unintentionally maximising a window can also lead learners to assume that they have deleted their work which is now hidden.
- Opening a new window on top of an existing one so that it seems to disappear.
- Saving a file to the wrong folder will leave new learners baffled.
- Opening a second file in an application on top of their work may make learners believe they have lost their work.
- Implementing keyboard short-cuts by mistake may start actions that learners simply do not understand.

## Input devices

New users may be very cautious with the mouse or other input devices. They need to be shown the correct way of using the device.

New users can have a variety of difficulties with using a mouse or other point and click devices such as:

- accurate positioning of the pointer;
- dragging the wrong objects, or the right objects to the wrong place;
- double clicking;
- clicking on the wrong object – users are then unsure how to retrace their steps, or in some cases they believe they have clicked on the right object so do not understand why it has had a different effect than they anticipated.

Users can find it initially a problem to locate keys such as:

- shift key;
- caps lock;
- delete;
- backspace;
- insert.

Users will sometimes press a key by mistake and become confused when actions do not follow their intentions (e.g. pressing the numbers lock key will result in a full stop being inserted instead of deleting a letter).

Users who have not learned to touch type will often look down at the keys rather than at what is appearing on the screen. This can cause many different problems such as:

- spelling mistakes;
- layout errors;
- enacting a shortcut;
- overwriting.

Users sometimes find that changing to a new input device causes doubt and uncertainty (e.g. touch pad on a notebook to a mouse on a desktop computer).

New users might press keys twice by mistake.

Users find the availability of alternative ways of carrying out a task initially confusing.

# Output devices

Users will sometimes be unaware that they need to switch on their speakers in order to hear a speech or other sounds from their computer. They are left confused by an application because they cannot hear the speech explaining how to use it, or they simply miss out on the sounds.

The availability of several printers on a networked computer can promote a source of confusion especially when the user cannot find their printouts because they have chosen a printer outside the area in which they are working.

# Applications and operating systems

Users find it difficult to distinguish between operating systems and application functions and features.

Changing operating systems or between versions of applications is often a source of bewilderment for new users.

Learners working on an exercise supplied to them by the tutor sometimes believe that the layout of words (e.g. words per line) should be identical – this can lead them to use line breaks in their text. It is important that exercises are identical to what can be achieved using the desired approach.

Saving to floppy disks is confusing (e.g. A and C drives, which is the right way up and how do you insert the disk into the drive?).

Learners will sometimes find it difficult to locate previously saved files because the application is searching for a different file type.

There may be confusion about where files have been saved to and what they are called.

Learners may have a problem understanding 'saving' – they can do it by rote but did not understand where the file has gone.

Learners may need reassuring about what they have to remember (e.g. do I need to remember all these icons?).

When demonstrating how to do something using menus obviously other options are visible to students. They may well want to know what the other things do, either immediately or later.

The tutor has to recognise a variety of mistakes, e.g. deleting a row of icons, opening a second or third blank document on top of the exercise. Learners will do what you least expect.

Minimising, maximising, closing and re-sizing windows require accurate use of pointer. Re-sizing in particular requires very precise positioning of the pointer over window edge to allow the double headed arrow to appear – the learner then has to hold the button down and drag the edge – the idea that you can drag all four edges can take a little time to absorb.

If a window is made smaller, a scroll bar will appear. Scrolling is often a new concept to learners. Scrolling to left and right can be confusing at first.

Moving a pointer in a straight line can initially be a challenge and learners sometimes select the wrong application or function when using nested menus.

Often applications will change toolbars and menus, depending on the task the learner is undertaking. Simply highlighting an object may alter a toolbar considerably. This can confuse learners who do not immediately realise the connection.

This section is based on work undertaken as part of a research programme by NIACE (Clarke, 1998)

NIACE and LSDA have been undertaking an investigation into the training of tutors who deliver the ICT Skill for Life curriculum. As part of the study they have produced a series of profiles based on the ITQ qualification. This appendix shows four profiles of the ICT skills that a tutor may need to deliver the ICT Skill for Life in different contexts.

## Introduction

Profiles are outlined for four different scenarios:

Teacher working in an institutional setting with technical support available, covering all levels of ICT Skill for Life.

Teacher working in a community setting with technical support available, covering all levels of ICT Skill for Life.

Teacher working in an institutional setting without technical support available, covering only entry levels of ICT Skill for Life.

Teacher working in a community setting without technical support available, covering all levels of ICT Skill for Life.

## Teaching Entry Level to Level 2 in a college or other institutional setting

### Level 3

| | | |
|---|---|---|
| Unit A: | Make selective use of IT (mandatory) | 35 points |
| | | Sub-total 35 points |

Select three units from:

| | | |
|---|---|---|
| Unit F: | Artwork and imaging software | 35 points |
| Unit G: | Internet and Intranets | 25 points |
| Unit H: | E-mail | 25 points |
| Unit I: | Word processing software | 30 points |
| Unit J: | Spreadsheet software | 35 points |
| Unit K: | Database software | 35 points |
| Unit L: | Website software | 35 points |
| Unit M: | Presentation software | 30 points |
| Unit N: | Specialist or bespoke software | 30 points |
| | | Sub-total 80 to 105 points |

## Level 2

Select up to five units (not including any studied at Level 3) from:

| | | |
|---|---|---|
| Unit B: | Operate a computer | 20 points |
| Unit D: | IT troubleshooting for users | 15 points |
| Unit F: | Artwork and imaging software | 20 points |
| Unit G: | Internet and Intranets | 15 points |
| Unit H: | E-mail | 15 points |
| Unit I: | Word processing software | 20 points |
| Unit J: | Spreadsheet software | 20 points |
| Unit K: | Database software | 20 points |
| Unit L: | Website software | 20 points |
| Unit M: | Presentation software | 20 points |
| Unit N: | Specialist or bespoke software | 20 points |

Sub-total 85 to 100 points

**Total 200 to 240 points**

To achieve Level 3 the learner needs to obtain 180 points, of which 75 points must come from optional units at Level 3. The individual learner needs to balance the units at Level 2.

# Example

**Teacher A:**

| | | |
|---|---|---|
| Unit A: | Make selective use of IT (mandatory) | 35 points |

Level 3 optional units

| | | |
|---|---|---|
| Unit G: | Internet and Intranets | 25 points |
| Unit J: | Spreadsheet software | 35 points |
| Unit L: | Website software | 35 points |

Sub-total (optional) 95 points

Teacher needs a minimum of 50 points from level 2 to achieve award

Level 2 optional units

| | | |
|---|---|---|
| Unit J: | Database software | 20 points |
| Unit D: | IT troubleshooting for users | 15 points |
| Unit I: | Word Processing software | 20 points |

Sub-total (optional) 55 points

**Total 185 points**

# Teaching entry level to level 2 in the community (outreach locations)

## Level 3

| | | |
|---|---|---:|
| Unit A: | Make selective use of IT (mandatory) | 35 points |
| | | Sub-total 35 points |

| | | |
|---|---|---:|
| Unit D: | IT troubleshooting for users | 25 points |

Select two units from:

| | | |
|---|---|---:|
| Unit F: | Artwork and imaging software | 35 points |
| Unit G: | Internet and Intranets | 25 points |
| Unit H: | E-mail | 25 points |
| Unit I: | Word processing software | 30 points |
| Unit J: | Spreadsheet software | 35 points |
| Unit K: | Database software | 35 points |
| Unit L: | Website software | 35 points |
| Unit M: | Presentation software | 30 points |
| Unit N: | Specialist or bespoke software | 30 points |
| | | Sub-total 75 to 95 points |

## Level 2

| | | |
|---|---|---:|
| Unit B: | Operate a computer | 20 points |

Select up to four units (not including any studied at level 2) from:

| | | |
|---|---|---:|
| Unit F: | Artwork and imaging software | 20 points |
| Unit G: | Internet and Intranets | 15 points |
| Unit H: | E-mail | 15 points |
| Unit I: | Word processing software | 20 points |
| Unit J: | Spreadsheet software | 20 points |
| Unit K: | Database software | 20 points |
| Unit L: | Website software | 20 points |
| Unit M: | Presentation software | 20 points |
| Unit N: | Specialist or bespoke software | 20 points |
| | | Sub-total 90 to 100 points |

**Total 200 to 220 points**

To achieve Level 3 the learner must obtain 180 points of which 75 points must come from optional units at Level 3. The individual learner needs to balance the units at Level 2.

## Example

Teacher B:

| | | |
|---|---|---|
| Unit A: | Make selective use of IT (mandatory) | 35 points |

Level 3 optional units

| | | |
|---|---|---|
| Unit D: | IT troubleshooting for users | 25 points |
| Unit L: | Website software | 35 points |
| Unit M: | Presentation software | 30 points |

Sub-total (optional) 90 points

Teacher needs a minimum of 50 points from level 2 to achieve award.

Level 2 optional units

| | | |
|---|---|---|
| Unit B: | Operate a Computer | 20 points |
| Unit H: | E-mail | 15 points |
| Unit I: | Word processing software | 20 points |

Sub-total (optional) 55 points

**Total 180 points**

# Teaching only Entry Levels in a college or other institutional setting

## Level 2

| | | |
|---|---|---|
| Unit A: | Make selective use of IT (mandatory) | 25 points |

Sub-total 25 points

## Unit 2

Select up to three units from:

| | | |
|---|---|---|
| Unit B: | Operate a computer | 20 points |
| Unit D: | IT troubleshooting for users | 15 points |
| Unit F: | Artwork and imaging software | 20 points |
| Unit G: | Internet and Intranets | 15 points |
| Unit H: | E-mail | 15 points |
| Unit I: | Word processing software | 20 points |
| Unit J: | Spreadsheet software | 20 points |
| Unit K: | Database software | 20 points |
| Unit L: | Website software | 20 points |
| Unit M: | Presentation software | 20 points |
| Unit N: | Specialist or bespoke software | 20 points |

Sub-total 45 to 60 points

**Unit I**

Select up to four units from:

| | | |
|---|---|---|
| Unit B: | Operate a computer | 10 points |
| Unit D: | IT troubleshooting for users | 5 points |
| Unit F: | Artwork and imaging software | 10 points |
| Unit G: | Internet and Intranets | 5 points |
| Unit H: | E-mail | 5 points |
| Unit I: | Word processing software | 10 points |
| Unit J: | Spreadsheet software | 10 points |
| Unit K: | Database software | 10 points |
| Unit L: | Website software | 10 points |
| Unit M: | Presentation software | 10 points |
| Unit N: | Specialist or bespoke software | 10 points |

Sub-total 25 to 40 points

**Total 95 to 125 points**

To achieve Level 2 the learner needs to obtain 100 points, of which 40 points must come from optional units at Level 2. The individual learner needs to balance the units at Level 1.

# Example

Teacher C:

| | | |
|---|---|---|
| Unit A: | Make selective use of IT (mandatory) | 25 points |

Level 2 optional units

| | | |
|---|---|---|
| Unit I: | Word processing software | 20 points |
| Unit J: | Spreadsheet software | 20 points |
| Unit K: | Database software | 20 points |

Sub-total (optional) 60 points

Teacher needs a minimum of 40 points from level 2 to achieve award.

Level 1 optional units

| | | |
|---|---|---|
| Unit B: | Operate a computer | 10 points |
| Unit F: | Artwork and imaging software | 10 points |

Sub-total (optional) 20 points

**Total 105 points**

# Teaching only Entry Levels in the community (outreach locations)

### Level 2

| | | |
|---|---|---:|
| Unit A: | Make selective use of IT (mandatory) | 25 points |
| | | Sub-total 25 points |

| | | |
|---|---|---:|
| Unit B: | Operate a computer | 20 points |
| Unit D: | IT troubleshooting for users | 15 points |

### Unit 2

Select one unit from:

| | | |
|---|---|---:|
| Unit F: | Artwork and imaging software | 20 points |
| Unit G: | Internet and Intranets | 15 points |
| Unit H: | E-mail | 15 points |
| Unit I: | Word processing software | 20 points |
| Unit J: | Spreadsheet software | 20 points |
| Unit K: | Database software | 20 points |
| Unit L: | Website software | 20 points |
| Unit M: | Presentation software | 20 points |
| Unit N: | Specialist or bespoke software | 20 points |
| | | Sub-total 50 to 55 points |

### Unit I

Select up to four units from:

| | | |
|---|---|---:|
| Unit B: | Operate a computer | 10 points |
| Unit D: | IT troubleshooting for users | 5 points |
| Unit F: | Artwork and imaging software | 10 points |
| Unit G: | Internet and Intranets | 5 points |
| Unit H: | E-mail | 5 points |
| Unit I: | Word processing software | 10 points |
| Unit J: | Spreadsheet software | 10 points |
| Unit K: | Database software | 10 points |
| Unit L: | Website software | 10 points |
| Unit M: | Presentation software | 10 points |
| Unit N: | Specialist or bespoke software | 10 points |
| | | Sub-total 25 to 40 points |
| | | **Total 100 to 120 points** |

To achieve Level 2 the learner needs to obtain 100 points, of which 40 points must come from optional units at Level 2. The individual learner needs to balance the units at Level I.

# Example

Teacher D:

| | | |
|---|---|---|
| Unit A: | Make selective use of IT (mandatory) | 25 points |

Level 2 optional units

| | | |
|---|---|---|
| Unit B: | Operate a computer | 20 points |
| Unit D: | IT troubleshooting for users | 15 points |
| Unit M: | Presentation software | 20 points |

Sub-total (optional) 55 points

Teacher needs a minimum of 40 points from Level 2 to achieve award

Level 1 optional units

| | | |
|---|---|---|
| Unit F: | Artwork and imaging software | 10 points |
| Unit H: | E-mail | 5 points |
| Unit J: | Spreadsheet software | 10 points |

Sub-total (optional) 25 points

**Total 105 points**

# REFERENCES AND OTHER SOURCES

Abilitynet, *www.abilitynet.org.uk/content/factsheets/Factsheets.htm*

Adult Learning Inspectorate (2005) *Handbook for Inspectors*. Adult Learning Inspectorate, *www.ali.gov.uk* (Third edition).

Alridge, F. and Tuckett, A. (2004). *Business as Usual? The NIACE Survey of Adult Participation in Learning*. Leicester: NIACE.

Basic Skills Agency, www.basic-skills.co.uk

Basic Skills Agency (2001) *Adult Literacy Core Curriculum* including Spoken Communication. London: Basic Skills Agency.

Basic Skills Agency (2001) *Adult Numeracy Core Curriculum*. London: Basic Skills Agency.

Basic Skills Agency (2001) *Adult ESOL Core Curriculum*. London: Basic Skills Agency.

Becta (2006) *Becta's View E-assessment and E-portfolios*. London: British Educational Communication and Technology Agency.

Cambridge Training & Development. www.ctad.co.uk

CILIP (2005) *www.cilip.org.uk/professionalguidance/informationliteracy/definition/* The Chartered Institute of Library and Information Professionals, June 2005.

CIPD, Continuous Professional Development Standards. *www.cipd.co.uk/*

Clarke, A. (1998) *IT Awareness Project*. London: Department of Education and Skills.

Clarke, A. (2002) *Online Learning and Social Exclusion*. Leicester: NIACE.

Clarke, A. and Englebright, L. (2003) *ICT, The New Basic Skill*. Leicester: NIACE.

Clarke, A. (2004) *E-learning Skills*. London: Palgrave Macmillan.

Clarke, A. (2005) *IT Skills for Successful Study*. London: Palgrave Macmillan.

Clarke, A. (2006) *Integrating ICT Skill for Life with Financial Education*, E-guideline. Leicester: NIACE.

Clarke, A. and Englebright, L. (2003) *Online Learning and Social Exclusion*. Leicester: NIACE.

Department for Education and Skills (2001) *Initial Assessment of Learning and Support Needs and Planning Learning to Meet Needs*, Raising Standards Division. London: DfES.

Department for Education and Skills (2003) *The Skills for Life Survey: A national needs and impact survey of literacy, numeracy and ICT*. London: Department for Education and Skills.

Department for Education and Skills (2003) *White Paper 21st Century Skills*, Realising Our Potential. London: HMSO.

Department for Education and Skills (2005) *14–19 Education and Skills White Paper*, / *www.dfes.gov.uk/publications/14–19educationandskills/* The Working Group on 14–19 Reform, chaired by Sir Mike Tomlinson, published its final report October 2005. The White Paper responds to the challenge issued in the report – how to fulfil the needs and aspirations of every young person.

Department for Education and Skills (2005a) *Harnessing Technology. www.dfes.gov.uk/publications/e-strategy/*

Department for Education and Skills (2005) *Skill for Life*, ICT Curriculum, *dfes@prolog.uk.com*, A1043.

Dutton, W. and di Gennaro, C. (2005) *Digital Inclusion: The 2005 Oxford Internet Survey (OxIS)*. Oxford Internet Insitute, Oxford University, *www.oii.ox.ac.uk*

Disability Rights Commission. *www.drc-gb.org/thelaw/thedda.asp*

e-skills UK, ICT sector skills council. *www.e-skills.com/*

Essom, J. (2003) *ICT Mentors*. Leicester: NIACE.

Functional Skills, news and developments. *www.totallyskilled.co.uk/*

Gagne, R.M. (1977) *The Conditions of Learning*. Orlando, Florida: Holt, Rinehart and Winston.

Garnett, F. and Shaw, M. (2003) UK Online, Family Learning Good Practice Guide, *www.helpisathand.gov.uk/resources/teaching-learning/family/*. London: Department for Education and Skills.

Gartner (2004) *IT Insights: Trends and UK Skills Implications*. e-skills UK and Gartner Consulting.

Georgiou, G. (2004) *General IT Literacy*. Swindon: British Computer Society.

Horsburgh, D. and Woodlock, J. (2000) Initial Assessment of Key Skills: Considerations for Colleges, *www.lsda.org.uk/files/pdf/ISBN185338609X.pdf*. London: Learning Skills and Development Agency.

Jacobsen, Y. (2000) *Our Right to Learn*. Leicester: NIACE.

Key Skills, *www.keyskillssupport.net/organising/specstandardsguidance/*

Kirkpatrick, D. L. (1998) *Evaluating Training Programs*. San Francsico: Berret-Koehler Publishers (Second Edition).

Kolb, D. (1984) *Experiential Learning: Experience as the Source of Learning and Development*. Englewood Cliffs, N.J.: Prentice-Hall, Inc.

Learning and Skills Council (2005) *Recognising and Recording Progress and Achievement in Non-accredited learning. www.lsc.org.uk*

Learning and Skills Development Agency (2001) *Agency responds: Skills for Life*. London: LSDA.

Money Matters to Me, www.moneymatterstome.co.uk

National Office of Statistics (2005) *National Statistics Omnibus Survey. www.statistics.gov.uk/*

NIACE (2005a) *And Now, Press the Red Button: A Guide to Media Literacy*. Leicester: NIACE.

NIACE (2005b) *ICT Skill for Life Action Research project Report. www.niace.org.uk/*

Ofsted and ALI (2001) *Common Inspection Framework*. Adult Learning Inspectorate. and Office for Standards in Education.

Phelphs, R., Ellis, A. and Hase, S. (2001) The role of metacognitive and reflective learning processes in developing capable computer users. ASCLITE Conference Proceedings.

Prime Minister's Strategy Unit (2005) *Connecting the UK: the Digital Strategy*. Cabinet Office, *www.strategy.gov.uk*

QCA (2005) ICT Skill for Life Standard, *www.qca.org.uk*. Qualifications and Curriculum Authority.

QCA (2006) Our Vision. *www.qca.org.uk/7192.html*

QCA (2006a) Ten Principles for Assessment for Learning. *www.qca.org.uk/907.html*

QCA (2006b) The National Qualifications Framework. *www.qca.org.uk/493.html*

Sadler, J. and Smith, J. (2004) *Boosting your retention rates – lessons for preventing early drop-out, Support for Success Quality Improvement Programme*. London: Learning Skills Development Agency.

Simpson, O. (2000) *Supporting Students in Open and Distance Learning*. London: Kogan Page.

Techdis, support for disabled learners. *www.techdis.ac.uk/*

West Nottingham College, bksb (basic & keySKILLBUILDER), www.bksb.co.uk